"A must read! What organization doesn't struggle with change? Greg Shea and Cassie Solomon take this daunting challenge from concept to tangible and practical strategies. Their 8 levers of change help us all focus our efforts to create meaningful change in organizations."
—**Thomas J. Saporito, Executive Chairman,**
  RHR International LLP

"This book should be considered essential reading for anyone who is trying to plan and/or implement change in his or her organization. It provides a very clear, succinct, and usable model for sorting through what change you are trying to accomplish and what concrete steps you intend to take to get there. In effect, it can be used as a more complex tool in the spirit of Atul Gawande's *The Checklist Manifesto*, since it encourages discipline where good intentions usually dominate. Once you read it, you're guaranteed to be more thoughtful about the change process and that should certainly translate into being more successful as well."
—**Fritz Steele, author of *Consulting for Organizational***
  Change* and coauthor of *Workplace by Design

"*Leading Successful Change* should be in the briefcase of every manager and not on their bookshelf. The reader is warned ahead of time that the size of the book is inversely proportional to its depth. I have used the approach that it presents over the years, yet I have already read *Leading Successful Change* twice because it is so rich. It contains the essential elements to all who manage a project, a team, a division, or an entire organization and who seek sustainable results. We have all heard the conventional wisdom regarding execution and change efforts, but how often have we been offered concrete advice that addresses the entire work environment from a systems approach? Shea and Solomon do just this in a well-written, concise manner that is both captivating for its frankness in demonstrating successes and failures in change efforts and proving that there is no small change effort. And most importantly, that it is the people who count."
—**Robert M. Weinstein, PhD, President, Robertet, Inc. and**
  Chief Operating Officer, Robertet USA

D0162376

"In *Leading Successful Change*, Shea and Solomon powerfully explore two critical aspects of successful change. They focus on a vivid scene of the desired future as the place to start and then offer 8 compelling levers, which in various combinations can make it real. Pragmatic tools, cases, and focused questions help a reader navigate the turbulence of our current environment."

—Thomas Gilmore, author of *Making a Leadership Change*, and Lynn Oppenheim, President, CFAR

"We at Performance Programs have concentrated for 25 years on enlightening leaders about their behavior and helping them identify changes that will improve performance. Shea and Solomon's book, *Leading Successful Change*, cogently presents the other piece of the change puzzle, namely on how to design systems of work to drive behavioral change. Their approach is not just fresh, it is concrete and practical. Leaders should buy this book, share it, and discuss it. Most of all, they should use what's in it again and again."

—Paul M. Connolly, Ph.D., President, Performance Programs, Inc.

"Myriad books are written about change management in organizations but fail to provide practical advice on how to move the entire system toward the future you envision. Through their Work Systems Model, Greg Shea and Cassie Solomon provide a comprehensive and practical approach to leading your organization through the often-times treacherous process of change. I've seen firsthand how effective this approach can be in complex organizations; simply put, it works! Anyone involved in either significant or incremental change processes needs to read this book."

—Patrick T. Harker, President, Federal Reserve Bank of Philadelphia

"*Leading Successful Change* is a blockbuster resource that provides transformational, yet practical approaches to implementing and

Praise for *Leading Successful Change*

"Few people have more experience guiding organizational change than Greg Shea and Cassie Solomon. Their book gives you a front-row seat to major transformation efforts—and a collection of tips that you can put into practice straightaway."
—**Adam Grant**, *New York Times* **bestselling author of** *Originals* **and** *Give and Take* **and host of the chart-topping TED podcast WorkLife**

"*Leading Successful Change* is more than a must-read for leaders today—it is a *must-use* guide for anyone who is faced with leading others to a future that is better than today. Authors Greg Shea and Cassie Solomon take a powerful and provocative stance on how change really happens. They start with *people*—who we are, what we need, what we care about, and how to engage our hearts and minds when we're faced with profound changes. Shea and Solomon understand that people expect and deserve care and attention from leaders, especially during times of change. In this new and exciting book, you will learn how emotionally intelligent leaders can use a field-tested framework to *engage* people in transformation that leaves everyone—and the organization—stronger and better equipped to thrive in our new world. *Leading Successful Change* is *the* book to read if you are a leader who genuinely cares about people *and* your organization's success."
—**Annie McKee, PhD, author of** *How to Be Happy at Work* **and coauthor of** *Primal Leadership* **and** *Resonant Leadership*

"Greg Shea and Cassie Solomon have written a novel and valuable resource for leaders of change."
—**Michael Useem, Professor of Management, Wharton School, and author of** *The Leader's Checklist*

"The financial service industry has been beset on all sides by structural changes and challenges to its business model. Rapid changes in technology, consumer expectations, and behavior have joined with confusing and increasing governmental regulations, all of which

now require financial organizations who want to continue to thrive to alter their businesses, the way they deliver their services, and the organizational structures that will enable them to do so. At this time, there is much more urgency to get the necessary changes *right* the first time, as the pace and complexity of change will not abide anything but near perfect execution. In *Leading Successful Change*, Greg Shea and Cassie Solomon have produced a wonderfully concise outline which will enable leaders to meaningfully engage in the visioning and execution of such changes within an organization. While the hard work of articulating the vision and implementation remain, the reader will have a strong leg up in the journey utilizing the tools provided. My thanks to them for publishing this book."
—**Richard J. Green, Board Chairman and CEO, Firstrust Bank**

"As the nature of change in the healthcare industry evolves and the pace of change quickens, leaders are charged with taking on an increased commitment to growth and change, to look farther ahead, and to have the determination to transform their organizations in the face of greater uncertainty. *Leading Successful Change* is a vital resource for anyone who leads organizational change. Gregory Shea and Cassie Solomon articulate a model for envisioning and implementing change that every leader can use before and throughout any change initiative. I highly recommend *Leading Successful Change* as an essential reference guide."
—**Steven M. Altschuler, MD and Managing Director,**
Healthcare Ventures at Ziff Capital Partners

"Bookshelves—real and virtual—abound with books and journals about the inevitability and importance of change. Now Greg Shea and Cassie Solomon have written *Leading Successful Change*, which describes the organizational challenges of change and a plan to affect it. This is an important read for anyone who recognizes that dealing with change is critical to success and is concerned about past ineffective efforts. Unlike so many books on the art and science of leadership and management, this one is without fluff and consequently delivers its messages clearly and concisely."
—**Hugh Hochberg, Principal, The Coxe Group Inc.**

sustaining change—taking out the chaos that typically accompanies most organizational change initiatives."

"In our turbulent environment, the ability to adapt and to change efficiently have become a fundamental requirement for competitiveness. *Leading Successful Change* brings the reader the benefit of years of experience in helping organizations to transform themselves. Consequently, the approach presented is most practical. This book should be in the toolbox of CEOs and top executives who have to deal with this difficult mission every day: Lead your business in continuous and successful mutation. It is in mine."

"In a clear and compelling style, Shea and Solomon cut through the noise and assumptions around change efforts to provide a behavior-based and highly practical approach to getting real change to occur and to stick in organizations of all kinds. I've been deeply involved in change efforts in multiple organizations and I can vouch for just the kind of approach recommended in *Leading Successful Change*."

"In 2020, change is no longer an option and as a leader, you can ignore all the advice you have been given about 'keeping the status quo as it is.' Gregory Shea's and Cassie Solomon's groundbreaking work on *Leading Successful Change* has been updated and transformed and, in my opinion, is the handbook for positive disruption for any leader in any industry in the 2020s."

GREGORY P. SHEA AND CASSIE A. SOLOMON

LEADING SUCCESSFUL CHANGE

8 KEYS TO MAKING CHANGE WORK

REVISED & UPDATED EDITION

WHARTON
SCHOOL
PRESS

*To my wife, Iris, and to our daughters, Emelyn and Meredith,
and to the remarkable grace that the love of all three has provided
me, especially through my recent trials and tribulations—GPS*

*To Claire, Katie, and Ben for teaching me everything I know
about real change and real love—CAS*

"It is not the strongest of the species that survives, nor the most intelligent that survives. It is the one that is the most adaptable to change."

—Charles Darwin

"Our ability to adapt is amazing. Our ability to change isn't quite as spectacular."

—Lisa Lutz, *The Spellmans Strike Again*

"You never change things fighting the existing reality. To change something, build a new model that makes the existing model obsolete."

—Richard Buckminster Fuller

© 2020, 2013 by Shea and Associates, Inc.

Published by Wharton School Press
The Wharton School
University of Pennsylvania
3620 Locust Walk
2000 Steinberg Hall-Dietrich Hall
Philadelphia, PA 19104
Email: whartonschoolpress@wharton.upenn.edu
Website: wsp.wharton.upenn.edu

Ebook ISBN: 978-1-61363-093-8
Paperback ISBN: 978-1-61363-094-5

Contents

Introduction
Why Change Initiatives Fail

J ack Dorsey returned to Twitter as CEO in September 2015, taking over the company he had founded and whose stock and user base had been faltering for the past few years.[1] By all accounts, the outlook wasn't good.

"In the Internet space, when things start to slow or collapse, they disappear," BTIG analyst Rich Greenfield told BuzzFeed News.[2] The most compelling part of Twitter's eventual comeback is that it came back at all. Usually, once a social media platform begins to lose steam, its end has already begun (think Myspace, Yik Yak, and so many others).[3]

Twitter has proved to be different. By mid-2018, Dorsey and his team had made an unlikely turnaround, as Twitter's stock hit its highest point in three years.[4]

Dorsey and his team had reestablished control by making a number of significant moves to strengthen Twitter's fundamentals, including "a directive to its product team to rethink *every-thing*."[5] How did Twitter turn itself around and become profitable in one of the most turbulent and competitive industries, namely, social media?

As you'll read in this book, our approach to leading successful change guided a significant area of the organization—the Customers Organization—and helped change the fortune of the company.

Change Is Inevitable

We once understood change to be episodic. We moved from a steady state through change to a new steady state. Change then became, paradoxically, a constant. As Greg wrote with Robert Gunther, we needed a new job survival guide[6] that would allow one to thrive in constant change.

Current technological changes continue to bear out Joseph Schumpeter's notion of capitalism's inherent "creative destruction" and the accompanying pressure on organizations to change.[7] Klaus Schwab, founder and executive chairman of the World Economic Forum, recently provided a list of changes in process: implantable technologies, our digital presences, vision as the new interface, wearable internet, ubiquitous computing, supercomputing in your pocket, storage for all, internet of and for things, connected home, smart cities, big decision data, driverless cars, artificial intelligence (AI) (decision making and impact on white-collar jobs, robotics, and services), bitcoin, blockchain, the sharing economy, governments, 3D (printing, manufacturing, human health, and consumer products), designer beings, and neurotechnologies.[8]

These external realities create a persistent turbulent field around our organizations and demand that we continuously adapt to them. Unfortunately, we're not very good at organizational change. Study after study, decade after decade, report similar findings, namely, that between 50% and 75% of change initiatives fail.[9] The notes for this chapter reference 10 such studies, from 1994 to 2019. More recently, McKinsey research found that 70% of change efforts fail,[10] and research conducted in March 2019 found that only 15% of global survey respondents reported that their organizations achieved successful culture transformation, pushing the failure rate for culture change higher, to 85%.[11] We need to get better at change—much better. This book, based on our experience and research about how to effectively make change, can help.

Why We Wrote This Book

The authors have known each other for over 40 years; we have collaborated in the changing of organizations for more than 25. We have lived very much in the trenches with those trying to lead organizational change. Many of the cases that appear in this book come from our respective practices and experiences, with companies you may know well: Twitter, Viacom, the Conference of State Bank Supervisors, and more.

We help leaders change their organizations in order to reach new performance heights or to adapt to a turbulent environment. In combination, we have done this work for more than 70 years in a wide range of industries: manufacturing, telecom, health care, financial services, power, information services, social media, government, professional service firms, specialty chemicals, and education. We have worked with US and international companies, start-ups and turnarounds, unionized and nonunionized, and with privately held, publicly traded, and not-for-profit organizations. We have worked at all organizational levels: shop floor, supervisory, managerial, C-suite, and board of directors. For over 20 years, Greg has served on the faculty and as director of Wharton's semiannual executive education course, Leading Organizational Change.

We've written this book because so many people invest so much in changing their work groups, departments, service lines, strategic business units, and organizations, and so many fail—at great cost to themselves, to their organizations, communities, and families, and to others.

Why do so many attempts at organizational change fall short? Certainly not for lack of advice. An entire industry exists concerning organizational change, one that touts an array of approaches: tell stories, make change a priority, "walk the talk," and ponder parables about mice and cheese or penguins and icebergs. Many of the most popular books on change address its psychological aspects and focus on people and their internal states or motivations—and they address both well. These ideas matter and can prove most useful. This psychological perspective taken alone, however, can promote the belief that the success or failure of any given organizational change effort comes down to motivating individual members of the organization and that, correspondingly, a leader's primary job comes down to inspiring the troops. Such a belief can easily lead to both failure and unfortunate attributions, namely, marking individuals as the problem. The individual employee receives the label "resistant," and perhaps the leader becomes stigmatized as "uninspiring." We contend that altering the attribution and recasting the challenge of resistance significantly improve the likelihood of success.

Nor is that failed change necessarily a problem of lack of commitment. You may have led a change, big or small, that failed. You and others did so much right: You did your discovery work, scanned your world, developed a sense of urgency, and physically felt the need to change. You made the case (over and over), delineated a strategy, and lined up the powers that be. The change remained uncoupled from the day-to-day operations. The change turned into a shadow of itself and then slipped away, leaving remnants, lost credibility, and numerous casualties. What was the problem? What should you have done differently? What do you *need* to do differently next time?

We contend that change efforts too often fail for two reasons:

1. **Leaders present vague and abstract change objectives.** They say, "Improve communication between caregivers and patients and their families" or "Increase collaboration." Phrases like these mean different things to different people. They do not specify what to do or how to change. They do not focus on the key aspect of organizational change: the required behavior of individuals.

2. **Leaders underestimate the power of the work environment to precipitate or stall change.** Many change efforts lack a coordinated approach to designing the work environment. Hence, one aspect of the environment tells people to make a change, while other aspects of the environment signal to people to continue to act as they always have.

We present an approach to change that focuses on the behaviors that you want from people and then designs the work environment to facilitate the occurrence of those behaviors. In this book, we first offer a way to think about desired behavior. Next, we walk through how to design the work environment using 8 Levers of Change, a comprehensive approach to creating a clear and direct objective and then systematically altering the work environment to bring about the desired change.

The ideas presented here derive from the Work Systems Model developed by Shea and Associates, Inc., which is based on systems thinking and sociotechnical theory.[12] Systems thinking considers how one part influences both another part and the whole. Like nature's ecosystems, work environments consist of various elements that combine to make a system healthy or unhealthy. Organizational researchers Eric Trist, Ken Bamforth, and Fred Emery coined the term *sociotechnical systems* in the 1950s, when they worked as consultants at the Tavistock Institute in London.[13] (Later, Trist and Emery continued their work at the University of Pennsylvania.) *Sociotechnical* refers to the interrelatedness of social and technical aspects of an organization. Once change leaders learn to be system thinkers, they can begin to see that some systems in their organizations facilitate the desired change and some inhibit it.

How to Read This Book

We will show how to identify those behaviors you want to see in place when your change is complete. We'll introduce the eight aspects of the Work Systems Model and discuss how those aspects can become levers of change. We next offer compelling case studies of change leaders pulling those levers in combination, often creatively, to defy the odds, break the failure norm, and bring real and much-needed change to enterprises in danger of being swept away by the swirling turmoil organizations face today.

Changing organizational behavior isn't for the faint of heart. It requires patience, discipline, even courage. But it can be done. It *has been* done successfully, time and again, following the approach we lay out here. And *you* can do it.

Some advice on how to read this book: Pick a change initiative you've championed, led, or were caught up in that didn't work out. Make some notes to yourself on why you think it failed, and keep those at hand. Next, in another set of notes, profile a significant change you would now like to make. Maybe globalization has created yet another threat or opportunity. Perhaps shifts in taxes, tariffs, regulations, or a political regime have cracked open, redefined, or closed off markets. You might need to act because a major competitor has demonstrated an unanticipated strength or weakness—or because your own organization has developed or lost a key capacity.

Jot down a few comments about the nature of the change you seek and why it matters to you today. Then, as you move through this book, consult and expand your two sets of notes. The book presents concepts and illustrates them with cases covering a wide range of types of changes in various industries. The cases do not, of course, cover every type of change in every type of organization conducted at every organizational level. They should, however, provide you ample opportunity to see the concepts in action and therefore to test the concepts in this book against your own experience. See if a likely more successful approach to your changes emerges. We think one will.

Last (and most importantly), to all the readers of the first edition of this book: Your enthusiasm led to this revised edition. Your comments have made it better. Thank you.

Chapter 1

So, You Say You Want a Revolution?
Focus on Behavior and Change the Work Environment

Halloran, a US-based specialty chemical manufacturer, had a Big Problem. The company had manufacturing facilities all over the world—Asia, Latin America, North America, and Europe—and sourced its raw materials from thousands of small global suppliers. Management had created a global supply chain so complicated that it all but precluded lowering raw material costs. To remain competitive, Halloran needed to change.[14]

Halloran devised a strategy. Tom Keating served as the Halloran executive in charge of purchasing, and he had a Big Solution to the Big Problem. Halloran would henceforth outsource logistics completely to independent contractor Straight Arrow, and Straight Arrow would create warehouses in various regions to serve Halloran's scattered manufacturing zones, transport raw materials to be held in those warehouses, centralize their purchase as much as possible to China, and carry the cost of holding the inventory close to the local manufacturing need. The consultants would manage the planning forecasts and maintain a three-month pipeline of materials. Halloran would gain a great supply chain, and Straight Arrow would get a new business model to market.

Keating confidently told his bosses and direct reports that this arrangement would eliminate the long lead times for material coming from Asia, increase supply chain predictability, and decrease cost by leveraging world-class supply chain expertise. In fact, many of the ingredients for a successful change initiative looked to be in place, and there was no question about the urgency, given global competition. Keating and the senior consultant from Straight Arrow went on a global road show to explain the concept to operations leaders in every region. They believed that if they showed leadership commitment to the program, brought a quality plan to the field, and communicated it effectively, everyone would see its merits and a smooth implementation would follow.

Eighteen months after launch, Keating's supply chain leadership team held a retreat to evaluate the initiative's success. People agreed: It was not a pretty sight. Halloran operations people thought the Straight Arrow consultants arrogant, often mistaken, and far too expensive. Allocation of the cost of the program went to the plant manager's profit and loss (P&L), but allocation of raw materials savings went to the corporate scorecard. In other words, program cost and program reward went to different stakeholders. In addition, local purchasing agents didn't want to give up their decision-making authority or relationships with local suppliers they had nurtured for years. What was the problem?

The Straight Arrow execs couldn't understand Halloran's foot-dragging. And Keating couldn't jawbone or intimidate either side into cooperating. Six months later he was gone. His replacement struggled mightily to overhaul the initiative, but to no avail. A year on, the global economy in a sharp downturn, Halloran's executive committee canceled the Straight Arrow contract and the global sourcing program. After 36 months of struggle, Halloran's competitors leapfrogged it, and Halloran had little positive to show for the considerable money, time, and effort expended. What had gone wrong?

"There was nothing wrong with this idea," one of the principals on the operation side told us when we sat down to do a postmortem with him. "The execution was a disaster." Why? Simply stated, the change leaders did not articulate what they wanted to create; hence, they could not design to achieve it. The change process was, in the end, not about software or inventory protocols. It was about behavior, but just what behavior within operations or at the plant level? This lack of a clear behavioral end state meant a lack of focus. A fine conceptualization of a supply chain at corporate came to less than naught because people on the ground didn't use it. Why? Because local realities argued against it.

We're Only Human

The human being is a midsize omnivorous mammal that has invested large amounts of evolutionary energy developing a big and complex brain. This brain enables us to scan our world and to fashion responses to it. We can work in the concrete and in the abstract, and we can construct complex social systems that allow us to gain the power born of large, coordinated groupings or organizations. We study and experiment and learn so we can alter our behavior and adjust to new circumstances. In fact, much of our conscious mind apparently exists to manage social reality.

These qualities enable us to adapt proactively to our environment. We are not the equal of cockroaches or retroviruses in this regard, but any creature that can prosper in tropical, temperate, and frigid climates, in arid environs, and in land dominated by water surely deserves the description "adaptable." To understand just how "adaptable" we are, take a look around you. The average workplace is filled with people sitting in cubicles or bent over laptops, trying to figure out what to do next. Motivational and behavioral theorists might differ on various counts, but virtually everyone agrees that human beings from early childhood on try to make their environment work for them. The smallest of children demonstrate this tendency to reach out (literally) and shape their world. Adapting and overcoming are central parts of who and what we are.

Why, then, is organizational change so difficult? Why do leaders fret so much about it and management gurus regularly produce new theories about how to accomplish it? The answer is fairly simple: Far too often, we forget the basics—in particular, that we are, in fact, big-brained mammals adapting to our environment, especially our social environment, trying to make it work for us. Like Halloran's

Tom Keating, we design change to accomplish great goals, to make sweeping organizational reforms, to seize expansive new markets, and to survive in old, shrinking ones. But in doing so, we ignore the reality that until we have changed individual behavior, we have changed little.

Change Is All About the Lead Dog, Right?

If a leader walks the talk and manages by walking around, if he communicates by crafting poignant elevator speeches and relentlessly delivering the message of change, then conventional wisdom holds that successful change will come. After all, just look at the lead dog— or ape or penguin, depending on the theory of the day: Yelp, bark, and whine enough, and the others are sure to follow.

That is all well and good for animal packs, and it helps with humans too. But by itself, the lead-animal theory is woefully insufficient for changing large organizations or parts of organizations. Leaders modeling behavior and talking the case for change can indeed help enterprises transform. But the corporate alpha dog doesn't sit among the pack. She appears only briefly, via dispatch or WebEx or the rare visit—something like Tom Keating's "road show." Soon, the appearance fades and the banners droop. The workers, the managers, and even the executives look around to see if their environment has changed, if the tried-and-true behaviors that made their world work will continue to do so. If they won't, then it's time to adapt. If they will, then why bother to change?

How, then, does one change an organization—be it a company, business unit, service line, department, or work unit? *By changing the work environment around the people whose behavior you seek to change.* Therein lies the key to successful, embedded, and sustained change: Alter the environment, and people will adapt to it. Utilize a species strength. To get different behaviors, design a different work environment—one that requires different behaviors. Then concentrate on helping people do what they do so well: adapting. Design work environments that inspire desired behaviors, and you have already won a large part of the change battle. This amounts to "pulling" versus "pushing" organizational change.

Think Environment

Behavior at work is "overdetermined." This amounts to a fancy way of saying that people generally do what they do for a variety of reasons. Changing what people do, then, should address multiple influences. Anyone who has tried to begin or sustain an exercise regimen knows that those simple, straightforward, and unarguably beneficial behavioral changes require other changes. The exercise challenge isn't in achieving clarity about the desired behavior—like exercising for at least 30 minutes four times per week. Nor is it in understanding the benefits, such as lower blood pressure and a healthier and probably longer life. Those facts often prove insufficient to drive behavioral change.

The challenge is constructing a world around the individual trying to change: changes in relationships, work, eating patterns, schedules, lifestyle, feedback or information, measurement, rewards, skills, and support systems. For example, join a gym close to your home to increase the likelihood that you will use it. Ante up, make the investment, and buy the right clothing and gear, including a bag to carry it in. Set an alarm that reminds you when to go to the gym. Log and measure your progress on a regular basis, posting it in full view. Invent small rewards as you reach various milestones in the process (number of trips to the gym) and outcome (duration of your exercise or decrease in blood pressure). Create social rewards too: Train with a friend or support group, post your progress online for your friends to see, organize a group of people who are committed to the same goals, or send texts to your primary care physician. According to John Tierney, coauthor of *Willpower: Rediscovering the Greatest Human Strength*, one-third of people who make New Year's resolutions will drop them by the end of January, and more than half by July.[15] Depend on your willpower alone and you will probably slenderize only your odds of success.

Simply put, a desired behavior or set or pattern of behaviors must *make sense to people*, not abstractly and not for a moment of inspiration, but each day, every day, as they go about their day. To make sense at work, the desired behaviors need to fit the work environment. They need to help people get what they want from the world around them. They need to work.

If you know what you want people to do, then how might you design their world to help them do it? The question seems straightforward, and examples abound of successful efforts to do just that. Let's return to the world of fitness. Fitbit has developed a successful business by offering an approach to weight loss and fitness consistent with the approach just described. Fitbit (like its host of competitors) is a lightweight device that monitors your physical activity, calorie intake, weight, and sleep. It continuously measures and updates. It also provides easy access to measurement information and the ability to download the data. Users earn rewards (merit badges) as they use the information to make healthier decisions. A user can readily acquire the necessary skills to use the device. The manufacturer provides online support, and communities of users have sprung up, providing both competition and support. In brief, a modest technological innovation provides the occasion for altering the user's behavior through a coordinated altering of his environment.

But (witness Halloran) altering the ground-level environment is rarely the first thing that comes to the mind of organizational change implementers. Like Keating, they envision impactful strategic shifts. Next, they fill in the mechanics that will get them where they want to be (e.g., holding warehouses or strategic partners). And finally, maybe, they give some thought to the on-the-ground agents of change (i.e., the workers) who actually hold success or failure in their very hands. It's only when the promised benefits *don't* materialize that those involved come to see that the entire change process began at the wrong end.

As one Halloran executive told us, "The model was quite vast: plants and people in different parts of the world, all people who needed to understand what we were doing. Every time we tried to roll it out in a new plant, months would go by before we came to any result; it became a self-fulfilling prophecy. The whole program relies on implementation. If you get it implemented, the dollars will flow. If you don't get it implemented, it will just cost you money."[16]

This book considers how to create an aligned environment that will drive implementation and embed the desired organizational change. Yet, simply changing the work environment will seldom yield the desired change. Rather, one must change the work environment purposefully *in light of* carefully considered and specified desired behavioral change. The mantra of "We'll know it when we see it" will most likely not get the job done. Rather, elaborate the future world. Use that elaboration to guide construction of a work environment that will generate a pull toward that world.

Guiding Change

To guide design of the environment, focus on the desired behavior. Describe what you wish to create with as much behavioral specificity as possible. Avoid platitudes. Phrases such as "increased inter-unit communication" or "enhanced field and staff collaboration" have a comforting blandness to them, but they almost always serve to blur the picture.

The market may have presented an opportunity or posed a threat. Your organization's behavioral practices or patterns may have enabled or hamstrung a noteworthy move. No matter the cause or the reason, organizational change entails changing human behavior and making certain key behaviors a reliable and regular part of organizational operation—characteristic of "how the place works." Questions for the change leader are as follows: What new behaviors must occur, and how must certain people act to manifest the change? What's the story (or stories) that you want told when people in the future discuss how you and your people operate? What's different about those stories and the current stories that characterize how your organization does what it does? And what in the current work environment stands in the way?

Changing organizations comes down to changing human behavior. Design of the work environment or system design, in turn, drives human behavior in complex entities such as organizations. One might argue that human organizations are systems of systems. To change them requires less magical imagery and Herculean effort and more careful consideration of just what a leader seeks to create with change and how to align the work environment to produce that desired, even longed-for change. To increase the odds of successful change, increase the discipline of thought, planning, and execution, beginning with clarity on what behavior the leader wants and the system changes necessary to produce it.

Connecting Intent and Implementation

To create successful change, remember these two tenets:

1. Focus on the behaviors you want from people.
2. Design the work environment to foster those behaviors.

Focusing on behaviors and the work environment that supports them does not mean that ideals, values, principles, motivations, and other more high-minded issues do not count. They do. However, a leader who focuses on behaviors takes advantage of the fact that behavior constitutes the most important currency of exchange within human systems: One does or does not do something—forward sales leads or not, look for customer input or not, actively collaborate with peers on product redesign or not. Behavior of organizational members determines whether a given change initiative lives or dies. Behavior is the connective tissue between strategy and action, between intent and implementation. Behavior also composes culture.

Successful change comes down to identifying the key behaviors that, if they occur reliably and regularly, indicate that a desired change has taken hold. A detailed, even granular, vision of the future can dramatically increase the odds of getting there, not by rigid prescription of an exact future and no other, but by providing clear directional guidance for planning. Abstract or ephemeral visions wrapped in corporate speak do not. A detailed behavioral set of stories from the future can clarify communication, motivate and direct action, aid planning, facilitate debriefing, guide revising, and revitalize by occasioning celebration of progress. A specific vision can provide local meaning, understanding, focus, and energy. Above all, a specific behavioral vision helps change leaders redesign the work environment to foster the behaviors and the change.

Next, we introduce a framework for constructing scenes that will help you identify the behaviors you want.

Chapter 2

Make a Scene
Envision What You Want

Göran Carstedt, president of IKEA North America, summoned his top executives to a large meeting room to share his strategic plan. They arrived prepared for a flashy PowerPoint presentation complete with charts and graphs. Instead, Carstedt told them a story about a mother. He depicted a detailed scene of her and her husband getting two kids off to school in the morning. She gets up, makes coffee, wakes up the children, makes breakfast, and so on. Then he paused and moved to the heart of the matter: "Our strategic plan is to make that family's life easier by providing them with convenient and affordable household items in an accessible location. Period."[17]

Carstedt wanted IKEA to enter the scene, to populate it with IKEA-supplied usefulness that customers would appreciate having in their homes as they conducted their daily lives. He wanted his executives to write IKEA into their customers' story in a way that improved the story for the characters that populated it. Brilliant! As Carmen Nobel, senior editor at Harvard Business School Working Knowledge, notes, "IKEA has made very clear choices about who they will be and to whom they will matter, and why."[18]

Clarity of purpose avoids wasting resources such as time, money, effort, and communication. No surprise there. The same holds true for organizational change. If the desired change were to take hold, what would you see as you walked through a work area? What would you hear as the proverbial fly on the wall? Hover over the flow of information or product or service. How is the decision making on any given matter unfolding? How does information move, and from where to where?

A change leader who hasn't thought through these questions hasn't prepared adequately to move to implementation—no matter how grand the change scheme, no matter how beautiful the flow-charts or how heartfelt the calls for "enhanced communication," "a culture of safety," or "dedication to innovation." Absent a clear set of end behaviors on the horizon, a crew that starts rowing but with little idea of where they should head will likely end up exhausted, dis-illusioned, and lost.

Successful change boils down to behavioral change. Change leaders need therefore to focus on desired behaviors. Easy to say. Intuitively obvious, perhaps. Yet doing so takes time and effort and does not come in the standard executive or managerial tool kit. Doing so facilitates clearer focus and crisper implementation and higher odds of success.

The Power of a Good Story

A list of desired organizational attributes can feel detached, mechan-ical, incomplete, and downright uninspiring. Stories, on the other hand, have conveyed meaning and message throughout human exis-tence, portraying the living reality of yesterday or today, or, in this case, the reality desired for tomorrow.

We advocate drawing on the timeless quality of stories to deliver focus, meaning, and inspiration, qualities heralded in management literature.[19] Our approach draws on multiple traditions, including Russell Ackoff's idealized design.[20] Our recommended approach also draws on research recently published by Greg and Wharton profes-sor George S. Day, which demonstrates the importance of operating narratives for understanding and for changing organizations.[21] The companies that led their industries in organic growth typically had growth-affirming narratives, while those growing more slowly than rivals often had prevailing narratives that qualified as discouraging.

The narrative alone, of course, is not enough. Growth leaders '
rate themselves from laggards" by focusing on actions and design
consistent with the model presented in this book. The stories we tell
provide textured insight into the world we inhabit—or wish to inhabit.

Lights, Camera, Action

There's no "best way" to imagine the future in order to tell its story.
However you time travel, bear two principles in mind. First, move
far enough into the future to uncouple yourself from the major con-
straints of the moment. For executives, this usually means moving
at least five years and perhaps 10 years out. For managers, two to four
years might prove sufficient. Starting at a specific moment and working back to the present produces more creative thinking. Second,
assume the world you desire has come to pass. This helps make the
unreal more concrete and enables greater, easier specification of
that world. Working from these two principles, the process that follows should help you find the desired future and the behaviors you
need to get there.

Envision a Direction

Start Big

Just because change is difficult doesn't mean it has to be timid. In
fact, bold change initiatives can prove easier to pull off than incremental ones, because they force—or *should* force—change leaders to
think system-wide and not just about processes but about the people
who implement them. As noted earlier, there was nothing inherently
wrong with Halloran's supply chain initiative. The failure was one
of scope. Keating envisioned perhaps half of what the future required.
He could see his supply chain working like a perfectly made Swiss
watch, but he forgot that the parts that would make it hum were
people, not gears and springs. Successfully implementing widespread
change requires successfully altering widespread patterns of behavior

across large numbers of people reacting to a multitude of cues from the work world around them.

Focus on Intent

What specifically are you trying to get your business to do? More local problem solving? A broader, deeper commitment to quality or safety? Ongoing refinement of production or delivery processes? Enhanced attention to product innovation? A dedication to customer service and intimacy? What's the end purpose? If you can't state it in one simple sentence, you're not ready to imagine what it will look like if and when it's achieved.

Identify Critical Roles

Which organization members will most contribute to realizing your intent? And don't stop with the executive suite. Think ground level, in the proverbial trenches. Titles and job descriptions do not matter; function and behavior do. Salespeople switching their focus from volume to customer satisfaction may provide the most powerful insight into the required work system changes. Or perhaps envisioning environmental service workers moving from pure maintenance activity to customer representatives will enable the most acute (and painful) analysis of the current work environment. Or receptionists migrating from check-in portals to point-of-contact client problem solvers. It's the future. Anything can come true.

Focus on Behavior, Create a Scene

Become the Screenwriter of Your Future

Imagine a scene involving key roles. How might an account manager interact with production or marketing in another line of business or in a different part of the globe? What triggers the interaction—new, readily available information? If so, then of what sort? Why does the account manager care? Why does the person on the other end care? Who decides on a course of action, if any? Lay out all of what transpires as if it has occurred and you are merely recording the action. To make the scene come alive, and to force yourself into its details, pay particular attention to the following:

- *Person.* Think about a particular person in a particular role in your organization, such as a purchasing agent in a local manufacturing plant at Halloran, a nurse manager in charge of a patient care unit, or an engineer in the scheduling department at the Chicago Transit Authority. How will the change affect that person's day-to-day job or even just a particular set of activities?
- *Flowchart.* Create a step-by-step storyboard that helps you tell the tale of the imagined change in operation. What happens first? What happens next? Who takes what actions?
- *Story.* Tell the story from the perspective of the focal person or persons. Relate the story in the first person: "I am a purchasing manager, and when I get to work in the morning, I have an urgent message from my internal customer in sales . . ." What do you say? What do you do next? Whom do you talk to? What information do you request and receive, and in what form?
- *Props.* Mock up a sample report, dashboard, or meeting agenda for this brave new world. The specificity in and of itself is not the point; it only serves to illustrate what tools, if available, will serve to support or drive the desired behaviors. For example, if you are a nurse manager in charge of an inpatient hospital unit, look at the data you might receive every morning based on a new tool. Having a sample report in hand makes it easier to talk with the "change target" (i.e., the owner and controller of the desired behavior) about just what the desired change is and what will sustain it.

Repeat

Focus on other key roles and do the same. Perhaps one scene involves a proactive middle management group fashioning the best approach to handling account receivables, another scene delineates an idealized performance review session for vice presidents, and still another describes a consideration of capital allocation or the desired approach to determining space needs. Build a portfolio of scenes as needed, and repeatedly share, review, and refine them. Make them living documents refreshed often.

Stay with It

Constructing scenes often proves the most difficult step in designing change. People want to rush to the work environment and implementation. Yet, clarity about the scene improves designing the environment. What does the desired future look like? How does it work? Get as specific as possible. Take your time. How you see the future has everything to do with how you will plan to get there.

Consider interviewing key stakeholders, especially those whose behavior must change, such as those likely featured in scenes of the future. Interviews can amount to guided visioning sessions as interviewees fabricate a scene that for them would indicate the living practice of the organizational change. Decision points emerge. Interviewees make narrative choices on the spot before continuing their story. They create conversations and action flows. Sketching out just one storyline can take close to an hour as interviewees choose who within their scene should initiate or respond to which type of client contact or who ought to direct a project meeting or when and who should mobilize cross-project resources. Each interview will have holes in the story, but each will provide a glimpse of what a living and functioning change could produce. The scenes derived from the interviews will likely not prove complete or constitute only one possible future.

Scenes usually range in length from one to four pages. They often include both actual and fictitious characters occupying current and fictitious positions. Some include extensive multiparty dialogue. All scenes should assume and reference supporting structures, workspace and tools, protocols, training, rewards, measures, information, and decision allocation *in use*. Scenes should not elaborate on the underlying nature of these work systems, only on their use and effect. Each scene should portray success but not necessarily in the same way or even in complementary ways from one scene to another. Scenes ground the look of the future and unearth contradictions calling for resolution.

The vividness of the scenes may well surprise change leaders and yield comments such as "We can hear our people talking!" or "This is us doing business!" That specificity and credibility improve consideration of the change and whether to pursue it. Scenes also provide the means for subsequent, detailed, positive communication of the change to others.

Two final pieces of counsel. First, you may well find it helpful to use an interviewer and writer to construct the scenes. Conducting interviews and constructing scenes benefit from experience with the process and from trust in the interviewer. Second, think about the Pareto principle: Have you depicted the right 20% of the change to make you confident that the other 80% will follow?[22] If yes, then move on. If not, then develop the scene further or construct additional scenes. Aim for enough key scenes to define the trajectory of the change and its behavioral nature.

Next, we turn to the task of identifying necessary changes in the work environment.

Chapter 3

The 8 Levers of Change
Design the Work Environment

S cene making identifies the end-point behaviors that will mark a
successful transformation. Detail in the scene facilitates effective
redesign of the work environment. Going so deep into the weeds can
feel overly tactical or detailed, inappropriate for senior executives. Yet
such specificity grounds the consideration of company-wide change
in the experience of organizational members, the people by whom
the transformation will live or die.

Actually changing what people do at work requires changing the
cues they receive from their work environment—cues they receive
all day, every day, whether a leader of any stripe stands in front of
them or not. Otherwise, even the best-intentioned behavioral modeling or inspirational address becomes a curious non sequitur. As
Confucius said, "The relation between superiors and inferiors is like
that between the wind and the grass. The grass must bend when the
wind blows across it."[23] The wind, though, can blow only so long
before it must move on—and what then? Then the previous environment returns, the old cues honored, and the grass straightens,
unchanged by the power and bluster that passed over it.

What constitutes people's environment at work? Our decades of
experience have taught us that the work system as a whole is composed of eight environmental aspects ranging from the physical
setting to available skills to rewards. Each aspect provides powerful
cues to organizational members about how to act, and each can
become a powerful lever of change. We describe the 8 Levers of

nge in this chapter and provide multiple examples of them in use in the next.

First, an introduction to the 8 Levers of Change:

Lever	Definition
1. Organization	Structure (vertical chain of command and horizontal means of interconnection); the organizational chart; also task forces, project groups, and committees
2. Workplace design	Layout of physical and virtual space; also available work tools and technology
3. Task	Work processes, protocols, and pathways
4. People	Selection, skills, learning, and orientation of the focal organizational, business unit, department, or work unit members
5. Rewards	Rewards and punishments of every sort germane to the desired behavior or scene; compensation; intrinsic and extrinsic rewards
6. Measurement	Metrics; scorecard of performance
7. Information distribution	Who knows what, when, and how
8. Decision allocation	Who participates when, in what way, in which decision

Lever 1: Organization

"Organization" conjures up lines and boxes on a chart. But organization is more than that, and how an organization is organized, in fact, sends off a constant stream of cues about what is expected and how to behave. Does an organization structure by geography, function/discipline, service/product line, market segment, or information flow? What is centralized and what is decentralized? Does the organization use a matrix structure? What about the number, nature, charter, and membership of scheduled meetings? Who attends them? All these sub-elements affect the work environment, and all of them can become levers of change.

Questions to consider when thinking about Lever 1: Organization:

- How might you change the organizational chart, including adding or subtracting positions or changing where positions report in the organization?
- How tight a coupling exists between which groups or roles? Who is "bound" together or split apart by the formal organization as it now exists?
- Would horizontal integration enhance structural support? For example, where might a matrix structure fit?
- What role might temporary or project teams play?
- What meetings or meeting systems should change? Should group charters or membership change? Which meetings should stop occurring?

Lever 2: Workplace Design

The arrangement of the physical or virtual work area; tools, supplies, and machinery, including technology and access to it; how closely (or distantly) people work together—these make up the hum of daily work life. Relatively small changes to workplace design can facilitate larger changes.

In assessing whether Workplace Design helps or hinders interaction, we typically ask if people have access to simultaneous email, collaboration software, texting, and/or videoconferencing. Proximity matters in human behavior, in both the physical and virtual domains. The closer that people are to one another, the more likely they are to interact. If we share the same coffee maker, copier, and lavatory, we *will* interact with one another.

There's more, though, and it goes back once again to the very social nature of Homo sapiens. We are built for face-to-face interaction with one another. For instance, some researchers suggest that we may have developed the whites of our eyes (an unusual attribute) in order to facilitate social interaction, since the whites help us indicate and perceive key aspects of social interaction (e.g., focus and interest) without saying a word.[24] Not surprisingly, the more that workers interact in person, the easier it becomes for them to use this distinct social perception to gain emotional intelligence about a given set of colleagues. Breadth of interaction helps too. One-dimensional interaction simply can never equal 3-D. Or speaking virtually, video-conferencing will increase my sense of you and how to work with you far better than will batch emails, but neither one equals sharing an office for us hardwired social animals.

Questions to consider when thinking about Lever 2: Workplace Design:

- Where might you locate people to facilitate the desired behavioral change? Do you want to recommend changes that involve people's locations (who works in proximity to whom)? How might changes to the physical space promote ease of access, collaboration, or general interaction?
- How might changes to the digital, virtual, or telephonic space ease access, collaboration, or general interaction? What role does—or might—social media, videoconferencing, or cell phone apps play?
- What tools would people need to prosper amid the enacted change?
- How might changes in technology affect how people perform their jobs?

Lever 3: Task

Pulling the Task Lever to create a new behavior can involve as simple an act as making a checklist of what needs to be done to complete a given task, or it might involve creating a standardized process. The tools of process reengineering, lean manufacturing, Six Sigma, and Total Quality Management (TQM) fit here. Laying out the flow of work *and* converting it into a formal practice can help make it a habit—the way we do what we do. Clearly delineating work processes carries special importance as we move into the digital—and soon the AI—world. Clarity enables both more detailed data capture and analysis as well as more informed insertion of AI into the ongoing monitoring, managing, and learning about the task or work flow.

Questions to consider when thinking about Lever 3: Task:

- What kind of work process changes foster the desired end state?
- How would the flow of the work need to change?
- Would it help to make more tasks, especially key processes, more explicit?
- Would more standardization of any processes help? Would less?
- Might the use of a particular technique such as Six Sigma aid in clarifying current and desired work processes?
- How might the flow of work facilitate digitizing the analysis of the work process?
- In what way might AI fit in the flow of work?

Lever 4: People

Of all the Change Levers, none holds a more outsize place in the mythology of organizational change than People. The People Lever dominates our view of organizations as well as our assumptions about how to change them. Witness common expressions such as "We just don't have the right people on the bus" or "I'm playing with a B team." When a leader thinks this way, the answer is simple: Replace the individuals or retool them through training or coaching, and the entire enterprise will change.

The point here is not to ignore hiring/firing or selection, training and development, or coaching when trying to change organizational behavior. Yet, leaders would also do well to keep in mind Abraham Maslow's famous saying "If the only tool you have is a hammer, you tend to see every problem as a nail."[25] Over and over.

We return to a point made in the introduction, namely, that much of what we attribute to the failure of individuals stems from poorly designed systems of work—that is, predictable and repeated individual failure rates by individual after individual indicate flawed systems, not necessarily flawed individuals. However one expresses it, the human and organizational costs associated with repeatedly hiring and firing individuals seldom end until leadership reworks the production process itself. W. Edwards Deming stressed this point, one resembling what the Stanford research psychologist Lee Ross terms "fundamental attribution error"—namely, that we erroneously attribute people's behavior to the way they are rather than to the situation they are in.[26]

Getting the people element right counts, but if you attend to it without also changing other elements, you will more than likely doom the change (and the people) to failure. The "new" people (hired or trained or retrained) will step into an "old" environment and very quickly come to resemble strongly the "old" people who formerly lived in and were shaped by the same forces. Systems deliver what they are designed to deliver, or to summarize Google's approach: Hire people who don't need support, then support them.[27]

Questions to consider when thinking about Lever 4: People:

- What would the desired end state require of people? Think particularly about which skills which people or sets of people would have to master.
- Which people or sets of people should manifest which values or orientation toward work, colleagues, customers, or other stakeholders?
- What changes in approaches to personnel practices such as hiring, reassigning, releasing, and training of personnel would facilitate enacting the desired change? What skill sets would these changes require and of whom?
- Are people sufficiently digitally and AI ready?

Lever 5: Rewards

The word *rewards* sounds positive, but the Rewards Lever works both ways. In work life as in other aspects of life, bad behavior is rewarded with punishment just as good behavior is rewarded with praise. What happens (if anything) to people when they act this way rather than that way, if they adopt the change or they don't? What does the organization truly recognize, ignore, reward, and punish? Obviously, money fits in here, but so do other forms of rewards (and punishment): intrinsic, social, recognition, and access (or no access) to resources and to power, as well as the ongoing experience of succeeding at one's work.

In many workplaces, rewards stand at odds with one another as well as with other Change Levers. Money may, for example, go to the highest individual performer, while social rewards go to the best-performing team. Or training may not develop skills that the enterprise rewards. Change Levers pulled in opposite directions conflict, generating competing sound waves that can cancel one another out.

Questions to consider when thinking about Lever 5: Rewards:

- What needs rewarding? What processes and what outcomes? What behaviors, practices, and scenes?
- What financial rewards would facilitate change? Think in terms of what rewards (e.g., bonuses) as well as their timing and structure.
- What nonfinancial rewards would facilitate change? Think in terms of both intrinsic rewards (e.g., rewards derived from successfully completing a task) and extrinsic rewards (e.g., public recognition of accomplishment).
- What unintended consequences of considered changes in rewards might arise? Homo sapiens quickly divine ways to garner valued rewards, and this can produce weirdly creative and unintended consequences.

Lever 6: Measurement

The axioms quickly pile up around the Measurement Lever: "You can't manage what you can't measure," "You treasure what you measure (or measure what you treasure)," and Deming's much-quoted

"In God we trust; all others bring data."[28] The sayings promote a similar message: You cannot manage yourself or others optimally or even well if you cannot measure outcomes or results.

Yet, we too easily forget that measurement is also a form of communication. It tells employees on an ongoing basis what management considers important—a message reinforced by the rewards that flow from high positive measurements or are denied by low ones. Align measurement with desired outcome, and good things happen. Misalign them, and an organization ends up pulling against itself.

Questions to consider when thinking about Lever 6: Measurement:

- What measures would foster and support the desired scene?
- What measures would help people to judge appropriately and accurately how they are doing?
- What metrics would help people manage and succeed in the new world?
- How might those measures differ from current measures?
- Should the measures focus on outcomes, process, or a combination of both?
- Do methods such as the behavioral or balanced scorecard apply?

Lever 7: Information Distribution

More than any other single factor, the flow of information determines the quality of decision making. The greater the flow and the stronger the current, the timelier and more on point decisions will likely be. The ever-increasing digitization of information allows its flow to more people faster, whether it's pushed to them or pulled by them. Employees, for example, should receive performance feedback as close to instantaneously as possible. How else are they to know which actions and behaviors they need to maintain and which to improve?

Questions to consider when thinking about Lever 7: Information Distribution:

- What kinds of information would facilitate the occurrence of the desired behavior?
- Who needs to know what, and when do they need to know it in order to facilitate the desired scenes happening?
- Who has access to performance metrics, and when?
- How real-time should the information be?
- What would enhanced digitization mean for the conversion of data into information? For its availability?
- How much information of what type should the system push out (e.g., reports), and how easily should organization members be able to pull it out as needed (e.g., intranet posting of digital files)?

Lever 8: Decision Allocation

Where employees fit in the process of decision making can powerfully affect their behavior. Digitization and AI affect the choices here. Digitization means that data can flow easily to any and every organization member. Determining who has the data (or the information extracted from it) is a key environmental design choice. Similarly, the increasing capabilities of AI include making decisions with nominal or even no human intervention. Hence, determining AI's role in Decision Allocation has become another key environmental design choice.

Decision Allocation cuts broadly across an enterprise, interacting with Task, Organization, and Information Distribution. Lack of alignment of these three Change Levers yields mixed signals, confusion, and frustration and greatly enhances the likelihood that even a much-needed change initiative will fail.

Questions to consider when thinking about Lever 8: Decision Allocation:

- How would people relate to one another when performing key pieces of work or when making key decisions? Who leads and who follows at what point in the decision-making process?

- Who would have what type of input into which decisions and when? Who has the last word, who consults, and who needs informing? Who takes the lead in spotting or attending to a given type of issue, opportunity, challenge, or initiative?
- Would formal review of decision allocation help, perhaps using a technique such as RACI charting (Responsible, Accountable, Consulted, Informed), from the Responsibility Assignment Matrix?
- Should some of the allocation be to AI, and if so, then with what human involvement?
- How does all this fit with Organization, Workplace Design, and Task?

How Much to Change

Moving any one of these 8 Levers of Change will alter the work environment in specific ways and send a different set of cues to those who inhabit that environment. But how much of the environment should change in order to drive organizational change? The flippant answer: enough. Ideally, future research will answer this question precisely, along with questions about weighting given levers for given types of changes, or how much which levers complement one another. For now, the answer comes down to this: Change enough levers enough for the owners of the focal behavior to perceive that the time has come to adapt to a new environment. In our best judgment, that means significantly altering at least four of the 8 Levers of Change.

Putting It All Together: The Work Systems Model

Thus far, we have advocated two tenets of change: focus on behavior and think environment. In the previous chapter, we presented an approach to envisioning the change you wish to see. This chapter has described eight aspects of the work environment that a change leader can use as levers to create and sustain the desired scenes—and thus the desired change.

Figure 1: The Work Systems Model

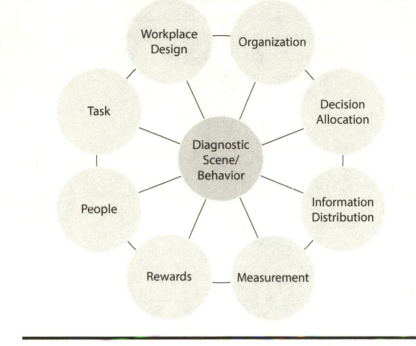

Figure 1 provides a visual summary. Behavior sits in the midst of eight systems that compose the overall work environment. We refer to this model as the Work Systems Model.

Check Your Work, Adjust Your Work . . . Repeatedly

Scene (or scenes) in hand, step back. Treat the scene or scenes not as dictates but rather as descriptions of desired end states. Use them to analyze how to craft an appropriate work environment. How should the work environment, as portrayed in the Work Systems Model, change to drive occurrence of the scenes? Carefully examine the levers of change and plan to change as many of them as much as possible in ways that will foster the scenes occurring regularly and predictably. Ask yourself if the changes in the Work Systems qualify as consistent and complementary. If so, then concentrate on identifying the necessary changes in the work environment. If not, then perhaps you have unearthed inconsistencies in the conceptualization of the desired change, inconsistencies that need addressing. Better now than later. Adjust the scenes or the portfolio of scenes as necessary. Return to this process as the change effort unfolds, checking and rechecking for alignment and leverage.

Chapter 4

It's Not Just One and Done
The Work Systems Model in Action

T he stories in this chapter show the Work Systems Model in action. They come from a variety of industries over several decades and illustrate multiple types of change. They all share one critical characteristic: success. They also illustrate an approach to change consistent with the one advocated in this book: clarity of intent, as well as significant and coordinated alteration of at least four aspects of the work environment for those people who need to change.

Creating a Unified Identity to Fuel Growth: Twitter

We began this book with Jack Dorsey returning to Twitter as CEO in September 2015, taking over the company he founded after a difficult period. Dorsey and his team made a number of significant moves to strengthen Twitter's fundamentals. Strategically, they focused on news and product improvements that made it easier for people to find what they were seeking. Operationally, they rewired major parts of the organization.

For the first time, Twitter aligned its internal and external identity around the idea, "Twitter is what's happening." If you asked Twitter's customer partners (agencies and brands) what Twitter was, they didn't know. Matt Derella, Twitter's global vice president of revenue and partnerships, said the company was "doing too many things and not doing any of them as well as we could. It's been incredibly clarifying to the organization to really know where we're focused, and that is helping people see what's happening."[29]

Creating a specific, unified, focused vision for Twitter constituted a "scene" phase on which leaders embark when beginning to use the Work Systems Model. Twitter's Customers Organization called the initiative the Customer Ethos and created a clear call to action for advertisers.

Twitter empowered its global customer-facing workforce to understand its new value proposition and to understand and articulate what makes Twitter unique. To polish the message about its identity, Derella's organization worked with Eat Big Fish, a global strategic brand consultancy, enhancing clarity about Twitter's unique value—"the most valuable audiences at their most receptive." Next, Derella needed to ensure that every member of his Customers Organization embraced the company's new identity.

To help him disseminate the new identity and focus, Derella turned to Meg Haley, who came to Twitter with years of branding experience at a larger global brand: Coca-Cola. Haley's charge, working with Cassie's help, was to ensure that Twitter's employees worldwide could articulate and embrace Twitter's new, focused identity.

"We used the Work Systems Model to think about how the effort could be impactful and coherent throughout the Customers Organization," Haley told us. "Whether you are representing Twitter in Japan or California or with brands or publishers, we want a single-focused value proposition to be communicated."[30]

To accomplish such shared employee focus would require multiple, coordinated changes in Twitter's work systems. "We were working in silos. After a difficult period where everyone was just hustling to drive the business forward, and communication between silos was inconsistent, we were ready to think about the company as a whole again," Haley said.[31]

She pulled the Organization Lever. Twitter's Customers Organization created a much more cross-functional way of working. "When we started, we thought we were speaking the same language, but we weren't," Haley said. "And the cross-functional teams are creating earlier and easier buy-in for these initiatives. These teams are building the data, tools and training that align with Twitter's new identity."[32]

As a baseline, Haley conducted a survey to see if people in the Customers Organization had a shared understanding of the way their customers use Twitter. She found that 80% of the workforce didn't share a collective, unified point of view. So Haley pulled the Workplace Design Lever and created better sales-enablement tools.

"Traditionally we just put together one global narrative and shared it at our annual sales meeting. Now we have started to roll out a much broader set of tools—case studies, videos, training, that are tailored to different markets," she told us.[33]

Haley also created a cross-functional learning council to align training across the organization. "Different teams were creating different training, with little communication between them. Each one answered the questions 'Why Twitter? When Twitter?' differently," Haley explained.[34]

Creating the council pulled the Organization Lever and the aligned training the People Lever. Derella's Customers Organization, along with Haley and her teams, also pulled the Rewards Lever, developing a rewards infrastructure, including the development of a set of sales competencies that help people understand the behaviors and actions that would be evaluated and lead to promotion and growth.

Twitter also pulled other Change Levers, such as the Information Distribution Lever. It strengthened communication between the various departments in Derella's organization. Haley created communication standards, including a more holistic central email newsletter for all involved parties. Leadership writes an opening piece about a customer experience, so all the different teams understand the way they contribute to the whole. They feature "drivers"—people who have brought this quality to life and who have embraced the new vision.

"Before, it felt like all communication focused on the direct sales team. The newsletter is an example of how we're working to ensure people feel part of the larger Customers Organization rather than just their particular silo," Haley said.[35]

Twitter also pulled the Measurement Lever, aligning its key operating results with its new vision and sharing the metrics with employees and with its board.

Companies like Twitter begin with informal founder-created systems and move to build the kind of necessary infrastructure that ensures the long-term durability of the company. While Twitter focuses on serving the public conversation and improving the health of the service, Derella's organization has focused on creating standard, shared ways of working that support its growth.

Twitter's Customers Organization took a holistic approach and redesigned its entire system of working to good effect. At the time of this writing, the company is thriving financially[36] and continues to attract people to join its team who believe in the company's purpose.

Implementing AI-Based Technology: The Developing Case of Preventable Blindness

The Work Systems Model can guide one's prospective consideration of change. The case of AI provides a powerful illustration, since its adoption often holds the potential to transform part or all of the entire system. Historically, the introduction of technologies such as the telegraph, the steam engine, the electric motor, and the computer "illustrate[s] a pattern of complementary innovations that eventually lead to dramatic productivity improvements," according to Erik Brynjolfsoon and Lorin M. Hitt.[37]

When first introduced, technology may serve only to run old systems faster, enhancing one system component. This is an example of pulling only one lever—Workplace Design—by introducing a new tool. The Work Systems Model recognizes that technology composes only one part of a sociotechnical system that includes multiple elements. AI creates the opportunity to redesign the entire system to achieve its full potential to add value, thereby making possible the previously unthinkable. Layering on new technology without transforming the underlying aspects such as workflows (Task), teams (Organization), roles (Organization, People, Information Distribution), and Decision Allocation means underutilizing the potential of the most powerful technologies to add value.

Dr. Robin Ross, an ophthalmologist and director of the Global Retinal Institute, says that "85% of vision loss is preventable, but it's a matter of detecting it early. And that detection usually occurs before patients have symptoms."[38] One of the leading causes of progressive blindness is diabetic retinopathy, a complication that affects blood vessels in the eyes of a person with diabetes. The blindness it eventually causes is almost completely preventable. Yet, a study published in March 2019 showed that only 15% of people with no diabetic retinopathy and type 2 diabetes receive the recommended annual or biennial diabetic eye exam.[39] These numbers become even more troubling when combined with the projected explosion of diabetes in the United States and globally. In the United States, the Centers for Disease Control and Prevention estimates that the number of people with diabetic retinopathy will nearly double by 2050, from 7.7 million to 14.6 million.[40]

Quietly, a watershed moment has passed. The Food and Drug Administration (FDA) in April 2018 approved IDx-DR, an AI-based system, to detect diabetic retinopathy and thereby to become the first clinically "autonomous" device, meaning that it uses an algorithm to analyze images of the eye and provides a diagnosis at the point of care without the need for a clinician. IDx was founded in 2010 by US ophthalmologist, computer scientist, and entrepreneur Michael Abramoff, MD, PhD. Abramoff said in our 2019 interview that "the health care system is totally unprepared for autonomous AI."[41]

"Everything has been done by humans for centuries," he said. "This concept of a medical technology that makes a clinical decision by itself, with no human oversight, was new for the FDA, and they were initially very skeptical."[42]

A breakthrough technology like IDx-DR can produce health-care savings while improving quality and patient access, or it could simply amount to a new tool in a specialist's tool kit. At present, a trained ophthalmologist or other specialist performs the screening, interprets the image, and recommends treatment if necessary. We know that by itself, the introduction of a new tool (the Workplace Design Lever) is not enough to change a system. In this case, barriers to widespread screening include lack of access to care and multiple workflow and system-level impediments, including protocols (Task) and reimbursement (Rewards). AI will repeatedly precipitate broad reconsideration of change-management choices as types of AI-enabled technology multiply—and not only for health-care provider systems.

The Work Systems Model can help a leader sort through changes associated with a potentially organization-altering new technology. At the center of the model resides the "scene" or new "behavior" that a change leader envisions. What future state does the change leader want? In the example of diabetic retinopathy, a leader may well choose the broader change and seek to deploy this technology in a way that dramatically reduces the cost of care and blindness in the diabetic population:

- Workplace Design: Any discussion of technology implementation begins with this lever. What tools are necessary, and what is the physical location and design of the work environment? In this case, the existence of IDx-DR can shift the location of care, which we anticipate will be a common theme. The interpretation of an optical scan that today a specialist performs in her office can now occur in a primary care office, or, potentially, in the workplace, at the mall, or in a van.
- People: Who does the work? What is their skill level and training? In this case, the work can shift from the ophthalmologist to another caregiver, such as a primary care physician or a technician with minimal training. Such a shift would require a mixture of new people, new roles, and new training.
- Decision Allocation: Who participates in which decisions, and how? Equipped with AI-enabled technology, nurses or

community health workers in the field could make decisions traditionally reserved for physicians in an office. In the case of autonomous AI like IDx-DR, the technology itself makes the decision.

- Task: This lever refers to the work flow, which this technology could also change dramatically, beginning with whether patients receive care at a primary care office, at a place like a mall, or even in their home. AI-enabled technology invites a complete reconsideration of work flow and practice and not merely the automation of old analog processes.

- Metrics and Information Distribution: AI can particularly alter the data and informational supply chain, creating new options for standard design questions. What information needs collecting (Metrics) and for whom (Information Distribution)? How should a change leader integrate the screening results into the patient's medical record and notify the specialist if the patient needs further treatment?

- Organization: What structures will we create to support the work, whether formal (team membership, reporting relationships) or informal (meetings, networks, informal communication channels)? What kind of organizational structure supports these new ways of working?

- Rewards: What gets rewarded or punished? IDx-DR faced a major barrier in the form of the legacy system of reimbursement for medical treatment. As Abramoff said, "How do you even get paid for this? The output of this device—FDA approved—has not been considered a medical record because a physician hasn't created it."[43] In the absence of an appropriate billing code, physicians using IDx-DR have been billing with an existing code, but that does not account for the autonomous AI making a diagnostic assessment. May 2019 saw creation of a historic new CPT® code for this autonomous AI, one scheduled to go into effect in 2021.[44] That change will allow physicians to bill for the AI assessment. To act locally at the level of a physician's practice necessitates acting globally to alter local payment and regulatory realities.

The case of IDx-DR illustrates the changes that will need to take place to leverage AI-enabled tools like IDx-DR. How will these devices be approved and regulated? How will providers be reimbursed? Aided by the FDA's Breakthrough Devices Program that designated IDx-DR for priority review, Abramoff created a pathway for other autonomous AI in medtech to achieve FDA acceptance and approval. He had many discussions with the FDA over eight years to codevelop the principles for evaluating AI, ensuring it is safe, efficient, and equitable. Abramoff explains, "They used a lot of resources to work with us because autonomous AI was entirely new for them."[45]

Additionally, autonomous AI poses unique legal liability questions, Mark Levy, partner at Eckert Seamans Cherin & Mellott, said at the Food and Drug Law Institute conference in May 2019.[46] Abramoff explains that "autonomous AI is something very specific. It assumes medical liability. It makes a clinical decision without a physician."[47] IDx-DR has made it very clear that the company has legal liability for its screening decisions and so pulled the Rewards Lever to support the desired change. In its 2018 AI policy, the American Medical Association advocates for companies that develop autonomous AI to assume liability.[48]

Finally, Abramoff has worked to create an entirely new payment system for medical AI, another example of pulling the Rewards Lever.[49] This is now mostly complete with the new CPT code.[50]

Creating a Culture of Innovation at Whirlpool

The case of Whirlpool demonstrates success in dealing with three common and often overwhelming challenges for change initiators: altering culture, creating innovation, and changing when not faced with a crisis.

In 1998, David Whitwam, chairman and CEO of Whirlpool since 1987, reflected on the daunting nature of organizational change: "This is my third time trying with brands. I tried brands in 1987 when I became Chairman. . . . The company resisted. In the early 1990s we tried the Dominant Consumer Franchise initiative. That didn't work effectively, either. So this is the third attempt, and probably my last. You see, this is a manufacturing- and engineering-oriented organization. The power base has traditionally been on the operations side, not the marketing side." In short, he believed this change important and he knew all too well its challenges.

As the world's largest appliance maker, Whirlpool did not face an immediate crisis. Whitwam, though, was taking a longer view. "As we look to the future, we realize that this is going to be a very different, very tough industry. Many people in the company think, 'The only way you can drive change is out of crisis.' There is no crisis at this time. There is no burning platform. But I've always felt you can drive change if you paint a picture of a better tomorrow."[51]

Whitwam envisioned a fundamental, strategic shift. He wanted Whirlpool to become the industry's innovation leader. To get there, it would have to develop a completely new set of organizational capabilities. Restated, Whirlpool employees at every level would have to behave very differently.

Historically, Whirlpool relied on just two groups, engineering and marketing, to generate all the company's new product ideas. These two groups "owned" innovation and divided it between them. Whitwam envisioned an organization in which everyone owned innovation and everyone focused on it. He enlisted the help of Nancy Snyder, then corporate director of the organization and leadership change process, to create an implementation plan that would spread innovation company-wide, soliciting ideas from all of Whirlpool's 61,000 employees so that innovation would "generate from everywhere and everyone."[52]

Whitwam and Snyder pulled nearly all the levers to change the culture at Whirlpool. In 2001, divisions needed to deploy 10% of their capital investment dollars to innovation projects in order to receive their full allocation of capital. The following year, the required percentage of capital rose to 20%, dramatically pulling the Measurement Lever.

Whirlpool pulled the Rewards Lever by tying annual performance reviews to short- and long-term success at meeting those goals. For senior executives, a third of their pay was linked directly to what came out of the innovation pipeline. For rank-and-file employees, the rewards were team based and not financial. "The reward," Snyder explained, "is recognition by your peers." She also said that the innovation challenge excited Whirlpool employees. "We had no idea how motivating this would be. . . . People at the bottom were saying, 'Finally someone gets it!'"[53]

Eliciting lots of fresh ideas provided a start. As Snyder put it, "Our CEO would go out and talk to thousands of people and say, 'We are going to have innovation from everywhere and everyone. If you have a concept, put it forward.' But we didn't have the systems in place to react to this."[54]

Clearly, a number of the Work Systems needed changing in order to support and develop the desired patterns of behavioral change this new strategy required. So Whirlpool pulled the People Lever and trained nearly 600 "I-mentors"—the *I* stands for *innovation*—whom Snyder described as being "like Six Sigma black belts. They had full-time jobs, but they also had special training in how to facilitate innovation projects and help people with their ideas. It's very likely that in your location or the department next to you, there's an I-mentor who you can talk to."[55] These I-mentors trained other employees, ensured the quality of projects, and accelerated the progress of project implementation. Creating this special function and offering a process for innovating meant that Whirlpool was pulling the Organization and Task levers in addition to the People Lever. By 2005, all employees were completing training in order to receive basic proficiency certification in innovation.[56]

To pull the Workplace Design and Information Distribution levers, Snyder's team created a suite of online resources called the Innovation E-Space.[57] This tool helps people develop a business idea, win resources for it, contact innovation mentors, and share ideas with other employees.

Before the change, Whirlpool's extremely conservative budget-control process had helped contain costs but tended to strangle new ideas. Like most organizations, Whirlpool budgeted annually, and once complete, its budget changed little, if at all. Thus, if someone came up with a great new idea after completion of the budget, no money existed to fund it. More flexible funding was needed to support more flexible, innovative thinking, so Whirlpool reworked the budgeting process, pulling the Task and Decision Allocation levers. Whitwam had each region set up a seed fund for innovation and told the senior team that they had to fund all the ideas that came forward, no exceptions. Whitwam also set up his own separate seed fund. He told employees, "If any innovator goes to their regional innovation head with an idea that the SBU [strategic business unit] head will not fund, they can come to me."[58]

As Whitwam pressed these changes, Whirlpool's senior leadership resisted. To break that logjam, he put executives through an "innovations champion program" and assigned senior leaders as sponsors for innovation projects, pulling the People and Decision Allocation levers. Whirlpool also established I-Boards throughout the company, with responsibility for nurturing and funding innovation ideas, pulling the Organization and Decision Allocation levers. Finally, by creating the seed funds and freeing them from the traditional budget cycle, Whirlpool placed authority over this funding in the hands of those lower down the organizational ladder—another big change in Decision Allocation.

Without a crisis, Whirlpool pulled all 8 Levers of Change and successfully embedded innovation into its culture. Its "innovation pipeline" went from $1.3 billion to $3.3 billion in 2006.[59] The emphasis on innovation has persisted. In spite of supply chain challenges, trade tariffs, and declining profit margins, innovation remains in Whirlpool's DNA. Whirlpool's 2018 annual report announced the launch of 100 new products.[60] "We are proud of the progress we've made in innovation and design, and our product leadership commitments were recognized in early 2019 by 16 International Forum Design awards and 5 Consumer Electronic Show awards," the company said.[61]

Sustaining Customer Service at Disney

Many people have "gone to school" on Disney's theme parks in the hope of changing their organizations. That's no small wonder, since Disney has nearly a 70% customer return rate.[62]

Indeed, so many companies came to ask for customer service advice from Disney that the company started the Disney Institute, a consulting business focused on improving customer service. The Disney Institute has provided consulting services for over 20 years and has counted among its customers a wide array of international and national organizations, ranging from United Airlines to 300 different school systems to the organizers of the Super Bowl.[63]

Disney's great secret? Precisely what we have written about here: constructing scenes and designing work environments to generate and sustain desired behaviors. Disney envisioned exceptional customer service. To create scenes, it borrows a technique from the motion picture industry: storyboarding. Disney designers create a three-dimensional world by seeing it first in two dimensions, as a storyboard, to "map the experience from a guest's perspective and improve and troubleshoot the proposed action before it ever gets off the storyboard." Disney creates the scene and then uses it to identify how to design its work systems to create the envisioned ideal customer experience—the "magic"—for guests to its theme parks.[64]

Disney employs many of the tools associated with the People Lever, such as a rigorous selection process and extensive orientation and training. It also pulls the Task and Measurement levers by setting and holding to rigid standards for how its employees look. Disney pulls harder on the Task Lever by defining the way employees do every aspect of their work, sometimes down to the smallest detail. For example, "one of the first things" that Disney teaches its employees to do is to point courteously, with two fingers or an open hand, because of the impoliteness attributed in some cultures to pointing with one finger.[65] As for scripting, Disney has invented an entire lexicon, one that designates employees as "cast members," customers as "guests," and rides as "attractions."

Disney continually works to improve Workplace Design. It studies and measures its guests and their behavior extensively and then uses that data to improve customer experience. No data, no change, seems too small. Consider the distance between trash cans. Disney discovered through study that customers, on average, traveled 27 paces with a candy wrapper before discarding it; hence, Disney placed trash cans every 27 paces. Disney provides electronic sign boards informing guests of the wait time at various popular rides, thereby increasing customers' or "guests'" ability to plan their day (Information Distribution and Decision Allocation). Founder Walt Disney's emphasis on setting (Workplace Design) lives on in the company motto: "Everything speaks."[66] Walt even mandated changing the texture of the pavement as guests moved from one area of the park to another. He insisted, "You can get information about a changing environment through the soles of your feet."[67]

Consider but one possible customer service scene: tired guests who have forgotten where in Epcot's expansive parking lot they parked their car. Tram drivers could help the weary guests find their car because the drivers started keeping a list of which row in a lot was filled at which time of day, pulling the Task Lever. The information from that process went to parking employees at the end of the day, pulling the Information Distribution Lever, allowing them to direct a family to the right parking row just by asking what time the family arrived at the park.

Decision Allocation at Disney blends tightly scripted encounters and considerable discretion to provide customers with a predictably high level of service as well as the most pleasant (and appreciated) of service surprises. In "Disney Service Basics," Jeff Kober explains, "The typical tendency for leaders is to try and map out all of the possible behaviors their employees should demonstrate when working with customers. This approach is flawed. . . . First, such behaviors come across as rote, rather than genuine."[68] Hence, Disney pulls the Decision Allocation Lever to foster exemplary service by encouraging employees to do something that we know gives most of us intrinsic pleasure: namely, aiding others. Disney encourages employees to take five minutes to individualize customer service by doing something nice for customers: giving a gift, leaving their post to take a photo for a customer (often of a customer), or replacing a fallen ice cream cone. Such initiatives break up the employees' routine and energize them, but more important, they can lead to this scene: a frazzled, worried, and disappointed family retreats to its room lugging a sick child and finds, to everyone's delight, a personalized get-well card from no less than Mickey Mouse.

Sustained, predictably great service comes from a comprehensive systems approach. "Companies come in and say, 'Just make my employees smile more,'" says Jeff James, who runs Disney's consulting arm, "but you can't take Disney and just plug it in."[69] As we've said repeatedly, to bring about and sustain desired behavior you have to envision, create scenes, and pull multiple levers in the Work Systems Model.

Really Big Change: The Portuguese Model and Drug Addiction

In the 1990s, Portugal was in the midst of an epidemic. Lisbon, its capital, was known as the "heroin capital" of Europe, with fully 1% of the population addicted.[70] By 1999, the country had the highest rate of drug-related AIDS in the European Union. In 2000, Prime Minister António Guterres joined forces with the leader of the opposition party and assembled a panel of scientists and doctors, led by Dr. João Castel-Branco Goulão.

The panel recommended dramatic, large-scale change: Treat addiction like a medical challenge and a public health issue rather than a criminal justice issue, and downgrade the possession of all drugs—including heroin and cocaine—from a criminal offense to an administrative offense, similar to receiving a parking ticket. Individuals caught possessing a 10-day supply or less of these drugs received only a fine, although dealers and traffickers faced prosecution and jail time. The world considered the change a wild "Portuguese Experiment." The policy went into effect in 2001, and critics predicted an increase in drug use, which seemed to be the case for about a year after the law took effect. Goulão recalled in an interview with the *New York Times* that "we were facing a devastating situation, so we had nothing to lose."[71]

In terms of the Work Systems Model, what was Portugal doing? Certainly, the Portuguese pulled the Rewards Lever—moving away from punishment to tolerance. One can pull any of the levers in the model powerfully or gently, and the Portuguese intervened powerfully. Even such a powerful pull on one lever probably would have proved insufficient. Regardless, Portugal did not stop there. The remaining interventions pulled almost every single lever in the model.

Portugal unleashed a major public health campaign to tackle addiction. In effect, the country took all the money it had been spending on incarcerating drug users and devoted the resources to prevention and rehabilitation. It pulled the Organization Lever by creating a different mechanism outside the courts to address drug users. It created a Dissuasion Commission, consisting of technical experts (psychologists, social workers, physicians) who perform an evaluation and assessment of a drug user. Recreational users might receive an administrative fine or community-service sentence. Individuals who have a substance-abuse disorder are referred to treatment.

"The best part of Portugal's program is the ease of referral to treatment," said Pedro Catita, clinical psychologist at the Centre of Taipa, a detoxification unit.[72]

Portugal pulled the Workplace Design Lever by taking its public health program to the streets, meeting drug addicts where they live rather than expecting them to come in for treatment. Portugal created mobile outreach teams, consisting of a doctor, a nurse, and social workers who urge drug users and other vulnerable populations to take advantage of shelters and treatment centers. The mobile units also administer lifesaving methadone, an opioid substitute, to stabilize addicts' lives and enable them to hold jobs. Overall, the mobile units qualify as a "low-threshold" program, meaning that individuals aren't required to abstain from drugs to use its services. Portugal considers the vans and the care they provide as a bridge to treatment for many addicts.

The Portuguese pulled the People Lever by staffing the mobile units with psychosocial technicians—workers without university degrees trained to provide education on such topics as safer drug consumption and safe sex. Using social workers and technicians allows the program to provide many resources at a lower cost, while also building relationships with addicts on the street.

The program involved pulling the Task Lever by redesigning the work process used to deal with drug users and addicts. In addition to referring users for treatment, the mobile vans provide a wide range of services: blood testing (TB, HIV, syphilis), syringe exchange to prevent AIDS, condoms, other medications (e.g., antibiotics), and education. According to Catita, most of these patients received no prior health care. Now they have access to primary care doctors, infectious disease specialists, psychologists, and social workers.[73]

By shifting authority over drug users from the criminal justice system to the public health system, the program pulled the Decision Allocation Lever. Goulão, now the general director of the Service for Intervention on Addictive Behaviors and Dependencies, said of clarifying the amount of a drug a user can have, "Setting a threshold reduces discretionary power from the police officer."[74]

Portugal pulled the Rewards Lever again by helping former drug users rejoin society, sometimes still stabilized by methadone. Rather than these individuals being unemployable because of a criminal record, the state offers them the support of work programs. Johann Hari, who studies addiction, explains it this way: "The goal was to make sure that every addict in Portugal had something to get out of bed for in the morning. And when I went and met the addicts in

Portugal, what they said is, as they rediscovered purpose, they redis-covered bonds and relationships with the wider society."[75]

Fifteen years later, it is clear the "experiment" worked. The num-ber of heroin users has dropped from 100,000 before the law was passed to 25,000 in 2019. Portugal now has the lowest drug-related death rate in Western Europe, with a mortality rate one-tenth of Britain's and one-fiftieth of the United States. The number of HIV diagnoses caused by injection related to drug use has plummeted by more than 90%.[76] The Portuguese approach also costs less, since it is cheaper to treat people with addictions than it is to jail them. The Health Ministry spends less than $10 per citizen per year on its suc-cessful drug policy. In the United States, meanwhile, the War on Drugs has spent $10,000 per household (more than $1 trillion) over the same decades.[77] Delegations from all over the world have visited Portugal to learn about its "gamble."

Today, they refer to the Portuguese Experiment as the Portuguese Model.

Chapter 5

When to Use the Work Systems Model

The previous chapter presented examples of how the Work Systems Model looks in action. Here we concentrate on when to apply it.

Discipline for Change Initiatives

If leaders ignore behavior as the critical issue, even radical transformations can begin to look deceptively (even dangerously) easy. Consider the following image. Greg's father managed in a company that fabricated and erected steel, usually in bridges and buildings. Workers regularly toiled at considerable heights to install huge steel beams that dwarfed the workers in size and weight. Cranes hoisted the beams, which swayed as the result of a confluence of forces. The swaying could have a slow, rhythmic quality to it, belying the power of its causes. Occasionally, a worker grew frustrated with the time and effort it took to get a beam into place, and he would reach out a hand in the sadly mistaken belief that he might easily stop the beam's seemingly gentle swaying and make it comply. Predictably, the worker suffered the rudest of awakenings to the power of physical forces at play as the beam launched him into the air. He received the most unforgettable of lessons—if he survived the teaching.

So it is with organizational change: Keeping the fundamentals in mind matters. A multitude of cues determine whether employees change or hold tight to old ways. Inevitably, the behavior of employees reflects the confluence of powerful forces. Aligning those forces through thoughtful application of the 8 Levers of Change in the Work Systems Model will precipitate behavioral change. Not doing so can well lead to an unforgettable lesson in how not to approach changing an organization.

The Work Systems Model (and associated tenets) helps guide and discipline the implementation of organizational change. Constructing and editing scenes, for example, pushes far more detailed consideration of a change, of what it is and what it is not. Maybe your response to a scene will be "*That's* what we want middle managers to be doing!" and you will proceed with enthusiasm. Or perhaps "Is *that* what we want middle managers to be doing?" and you'll have to go back and think through the scene again. Either way, the process leads naturally to a second set of considerations: "Why do people predictably and frustratingly *not* do what we say we want them to do? Let's go lever by lever to discern what messages we are actually sending about what we want." The Work Systems Model takes time and effort, but little wastes as much time and effort as a failed change initiative. Disciplined design of change constitutes time well spent, and returning to the model throughout a change initiative provides ongoing discipline for refining and advancing the initiative.

Deciding to Proceed with a Change Initiative or Not

Perhaps the most difficult decision that confronts many change leaders comes down to "pursue the change or not." The Work Systems Model is invaluable here. If you cannot change the equivalent of four Change Levers significantly, then don't bother. Stop and try something else. If someone else wishes to pursue such a change, then use the Work Systems Model to help him make the "go/no go" choice. Share the model or at least its logic. Ideas for change initiatives abound, but someone has to make an informed choice about opening and closing the spigot of organizational change.

In particular, the model guides thinking about what work system changes need to occur. That thinking grounds analysis of which stakeholders most need to support the change and in what way. The analysis can identify the resources necessary to alter the work systems that will drive the desired changes in patterns of behavior. In that way, the analysis facilitates determining who most needs to populate a coalition for change.

The Work Systems Model facilitates identifying which stakeholders hold the keys to successful implementation. The identified levers of change indicate which systems and therefore which systems owners and operators will most need to support the change and in what ways. Perhaps those stakeholders live in IT or HR or facilities or at the hospital bedside. Not having them lined up will likely spell doom for the change initiative.

Commitment to Change

Commitment to change seldom comes easily. Even people with serious heart disease often struggle mightily with committing to change despite the high stakes involved, including quality of life and mortality itself. "If you look at people after coronary-artery bypass grafting two years later, 90% of them have not changed their lifestyle," said Dr. Edward Miller, former dean of the medical school and CEO of the hospital at Johns Hopkins. "And that's been studied over and over and over again. . . . Even though they know they have a very bad disease and they know they should change their lifestyle, for whatever reason, they can't."[78]

By contrast, 87% of the patients who enroll in Dean Ornish's Program for Reversing Heart Disease stick with the program. In a study conducted with 4,000 patients in 2011 by Highmark Blue Cross Blue Shield in Pennsylvania, 96% of patients reported improvement in severity of angina (chest pain) after one year.[79] Ornish believes that people often find radical, comprehensive, sweeping changes easier than small, incremental ones. This is partly because patients who go on the "tough, radical," and comprehensive Ornish program see much quicker results than those who try, and largely fail, to make more incremental change.

"These rapid improvements are a powerful motivator," Ornish says. "When people who have had so much chest pain that they can't work, or make love, or even walk across the street without intense suffering find that they are able to do all of those things without pain in only a few weeks, then they often say, 'These are choices worth making.'"[80] The very intense Ornish program encourages personal commitment because it demonstrably improves people's lives.

Personal commitment in the case of organizational change has several components. For those whose behavior constitutes the target of change, it needs to make sense to people and not merely in some abstract, corporate-speak fashion. The behavior change needs to help people adapt to their world. People make changes that work for them. Change leaders should alter the work systems environment and then assist people in adapting to it.

In organizations, people evaluate a leader's commitment to change as they consider their own. Why commit to change and invest the required time and effort if leaders seem uncommitted themselves? Consequently, change leaders need to demonstrate their commitment first. People harbor understandable and justifiable skepticism about change initiatives. They have most likely experienced failure of organizational change efforts even if they have not read the studies. Failed change has burned them before. Consider the relative power of two demonstrations of commitment.

One leader visits every location, announcing and stressing the need for increased standardization of processes to drive cost down and quality up. A second leader makes no visits or speeches but employs the Work Systems Model. Members of the organization cannot help but notice a set of aligned changes in their work environment: a new organization chart; alteration of workspace design in conjunction with delineation of standard work processes; a schedule for training in lean manufacturing; reward and recognition programs based on new measurements of standardization, cost, and quality; enhanced access to data on cost, quality, and variation; and altered decision allocation along work processes rather than within traditional silos. Which leader has more effectively communicated both what the change is *and* her commitment to it?

By making meaningful shifts in the workplace environment, the second leader has more powerfully demonstrated commitment to the change today and then each day thereafter. This leader "went first." She built her commitment into the everyday messages that people receive from their environment about what their work is and how to go about it. She also set the stage for early successes by organizational members who adapt to the new environment. These early adapters, in turn, will do better faster, and their commitment to the change will grow.

Sustainable Change

Many a change leader has bemoaned the temporary nature of many an organizational change. A concerted push and massing of attention get the proverbial ball rolling—but not for long. If a temporary change is the aim, then such a fade does not matter, and certainly no change will last forever. As Plato wrote, "All is flux, nothing stays still."[81] However, most change leaders seek to establish significant change efforts solidly enough that they will endure, prove self-sustaining, and require a concerted effort to *undo*.

The odds for relapsing and recidivism in most forms go up absent changing a person's environment. Not surprisingly, the same holds at work. Building a work environment that supports desired change helps both launch the change and secure it. Recall Disney. Coordinating Change Levers not only supports changing behavior but also serves to secure it by making the desired behavior effectively adaptive to the new environment and thereby making more sense than other behaviors, including older behaviors. Hence, as long as the levers stay in place, so, too, should the desired change, and that equals sustainable change.

The Connective Tissue That Gets Strategy Implemented

Book after book, article after article, presents approaches to strategy. The continued outpouring of this writing indicates the ongoing interest in how to devise strategy, but as Cynthia Montgomery, Harvard's Timken Professor of Business, states, "Most notably, strategy became more about formulation than implementation, and more about getting the analysis right at the outset than living with a strategy over time."[82] The highly checkered record of successful strategy implementation supports Montgomery's claim. A devotee of this stream of work can read long and carefully without encountering a focus on the behavioral implications of strategic choices. Yet to ignore that reality in framing and designing strategy implementation seems at least curious and more likely dangerous.

Approaches to organizational change abound. Holman, Devane, Cady, and associates note that they cover over 60 change methods in their second edition compared with 18 in the first edition.[83] Nonetheless, embracing the notion that strategic change necessitates behavioral change means doing as we have advised in this book. First, construct scenes of desired patterns of behavior in order to ground the discussion of implementation and enable clearer communication of its intent. Second, review which Change Levers will drive those behavioral changes. Use this review to guide time and resource allocation and to sharpen discussion of such pivotal strategic questions as, Can we actually pull this off? In summary, the Work Systems Model connects the strategic intent with the challenge of strategic implementation and the organizational realities of change, a key connection and one too often weakly made.

Mergers and Acquisitions: Achieving the Benefits of Scale

Viacom began life in 1952 as a conglomerate named CBS Films. The name Viacom appeared in 1970. The organization's many twists and turns include 16 acquisitions from 1985 onward, beginning with MTV. Multibillion-dollar acquisitions came in 1993 (Paramount) and 2003 (Comedy Central). Thirteen of the acquisitions came after 2000 and seven in the past decade, with Pluto TV being the most recent (2019). Performance proved increasingly elusive for key assembled parts as well as the corporate whole.[84]

Bob Bakish became Viacom's CEO in December 2016. He had worked at the company since 1997 and most recently led its international division. Now, the once mighty media giant was severely challenged. Bakish's predecessor, Philippe Dauman, had recently stepped down as part of an ongoing legal dispute over Viacom's underperformance. The company faced a debt problem, and its movie studio, Paramount Pictures, had just posted a $445 million annual loss. Its stock price had plunged nearly 50% in the previous two years. Morale was at an all-time low. Bakish described the lack of leadership vision: "The biggest issue I saw, as if there weren't enough problems, was that there was essentially no plan."[85]

Viacom, as Bakish noted, needed a strategic plan, and he needed to retool Viacom for the digital age. Years spent working in silos handicapped the company by limiting its ability to leverage its size. Bakish needed to promote better ways of working across Viacom's core brands: MTV, Nickelodeon, Nick Jr., Comedy Central, BET, and Paramount Network. To create a cross-brand strategy, Bakish pulled the Organization Lever and assembled a set of task forces made up of representatives from Viacom's various brands. With their input for desired outcomes and areas of change, he and his senior team created a strategy to unify the company.

They pulled the Organization Lever again by creating network groups, such as Viacom Digital Studios, that cut across all Viacom's brands. Janice Gatti, vice president of communications and culture at Viacom International Media Networks, remembers that "Bob instituted senior team meetings to bring the brand presidents together to collaborate. Within my function, we now have regular senior communications team meetings where we work together to identify intersections between our brands."[86]

Creating a new meeting system exemplifies pulling the Organization Lever. Bakish also pulled the Rewards Lever, as the reorganization created matrix reporting lines and aligned bonus compensation to reinforce the behavior of working across silos.

Working together across brand silos meant changing the way people work together, pulling the Task Lever. And it clarified how decisions are made, pulling the Decision Allocation Lever.

"Lots of things are easier to do when you work in a silo; it's clear who is in charge. When you work across silos, it's important to understand where decisions are going to be made," said Julia Phelps, the company's first-ever executive vice president of communications, culture, and marketing. "The ultimate output is a lot better, but it can take longer to get there."[87]

For example, creating a cobranded film required figuring out new ways of working together. Does the power lie with the studio? With the brand managers? Who has the ultimate say? A joint decision-making process emerged for these new projects.

Bakish viewed culture and morale as central to turning around Viacom's performance. "It was clear to me that our culture, like the business itself, was in need of a turnaround and an evolution," Bakish said. "At Viacom, the culture had always been a real point of pride and a competitive advantage for us. We needed to bring that spirit of creativity back. We needed to evolve the culture."[88] Consequently, he pulled the People and the Organization levers to signal the importance he placed on culture by appointing Phelps to the new role.

Gatti recalled the importance of that change and the way Viacom handled internal communications. Viacom pulled the Information Distribution Lever with emphasis.

"We wanted to open up the communications by giving direct access to Bob, so staff could understand his vision and understand him as a leader," she said. "We launched 'Bob Live' for the first time on December 14, two days after Bob was appointed CEO. Bob talked very candidly about the challenges Viacom was facing."[89]

The company uses Workplace (a Facebook product) to livestream the Bob Live discussion to employees all over the world. Bob Live events continue quarterly and include watch parties in Viacom's offices (17 in the United States alone) with questions coming from people in the room as well as remotely.

Previously, internal communications to Viacom's 10,000 employees largely consisted of one email each quarter tied to the company's earnings reports. Those working in one brand probably had little, if any, knowledge of what went on in any other part of the company. Viacom created "That's What's Up," a weekly email that features five "wins" from around the company, to send one unified Viacom message on an ongoing basis. The team also created a regular video communication called "5 Questions With," featuring interviews with people throughout the company, at varying levels, chosen for doing something interesting or innovative. And Viacom created "Going Up," a video series interviewing people who were quite literally going up—in elevators in Viacom offices around the world, talking about the company's culture and reacting to companywide events.

Information flowed through every screen in Viacom's buildings, now programmed like a TV channel to reinforce messages about strategy, values, and the Viacom culture. "Very intentionally, we blurred the line between internal and external communication," Phelps said. "We were intentional about posting everything we were doing on social media, thinking that if our employees are excited, it's good for the external world to see that. And having our employees read positive things about the company externally was good for morale."[90]

Relatedly, the Viacom team also pulled the Workplace Design Lever when it created a tool, the Viacom Brand Book, which provides employees with clear language about Viacom as a unified company. The book, which is updated quarterly, emphasizes Viacom's mission, vision, values, and culture. The team also created manager discussion guides, ensuring that the message would cascade down through and across the organization.

One of the boldest initiatives was a three-day "multi-market next-generation town hall" event called Spark, created to reinforce the new, shared Viacom culture.

"We had to revamp internal communications to be modern and multi-platform. We wanted it to feel true to who we are, so as a creative company, we shied away from doing anything that felt too corporate," Phelps said.[91]

To market the event to employees beforehand, everyone received a badge that unlocked an augmented reality/virtual reality (AR/VR) experience promoting Spark. Across three days, over half of Viacom's employees participated in Spark. A global core curriculum around Viacom's new mission, vision, and values; cross-company panels; discussions about the future of content streaming; product demos; and skill-building sessions took place at over 40 Viacom offices around the world and were livestreamed globally. During the event, Viacom employees shared 500 million social impressions about their experience at Spark.

"The energy and the excitement of Spark was incredible. We ended it with a party on the last night that was attended by thousands of people. It was a cultural moment and a statement," Phelps said.

Afterward, Viacom conducted an evaluation survey: 82% of Spark participants said they better understood Viacom's strategy, and 70% of them said they better understood how Viacom's values guide its work. The Spark town halls will now occur every year.

Company performance provides the ultimate measure of success for any change initiative and, in this case, of creating value from mergers and acquisitions. As of this writing, Paramount Pictures has grown operating income for 10 straight quarters, MTV's performance has completely turned around, and Viacom's distribution business, which was experiencing problems, has renewed more than 80% of its business. In August 2019, Viacom and CBS announced their intention to merge, reuniting the two halves of the Redstone family's media empire.

The CEO of the merged entity? Bob Bakish.[92]

A Practical Approach to Cultural Change

Of all organizational changes, cultural change may well receive the most press. It certainly has a high record of failure. According to research conducted in March 2019 by the Institute for Corporate Productivity, only 15% of global survey respondents reported that their organizations achieved successful culture transformations.[93] Other studies relate a similar tale. The problem is that so many cultural change initiatives have it backward. Too often, organizations approach culture as if it existed separately from the work environment within the organization. Typically, anthropological analysis identifies norms and values; surveys and workshops produce carefully crafted lists of new, more desirable norms and values; and proselytizing ensues—along with "appropriate" reeducation interventions. The Work Systems Model points cultural change leaders in a different and more useful direction.

Cultural change requires altering "the way we do what we do," but leaders too often focus on the culture and not behavior even though behavior, adaptive to the environment, drives culture. No less an expert than Edgar Schein, arguably the founder of the formal study of organizational culture, writes: "The change goal must be defined concretely in behavioral terms not as 'culture change.' . . . One of the biggest mistakes that leaders make when they undertake change initiatives is to be vague about their change goals and to assume that 'culture change' would be needed. When someone asks me to help him or her with a 'culture-change program,' my most important initial question is 'What do you mean? Can you explain your goals without using the word *culture*?'"[94]

If one successfully applies the Work Systems Model, by definition, one will have changed culture—not because that necessarily constituted your original intent or focus but because what *defines* culture (namely, patterns of behavior) will have changed.

In July 2017, the Conference of State Bank Supervisors (CSBS) received the results from its culture survey. The assessment confirmed that it was doing some things very well and that opportunities for improvement existed, particularly concerning decision making and prioritization. As Kelly Haire, CSBS's senior vice president of human capital, explained, "Two areas of the assessment revealed that we needed to focus on decision making and prioritization. There was wide agreement that our decision process is too slow, sometimes unclear and that decisions seem to be made higher up than necessary. Another area we needed to address is that we have too many competing priorities and this creates confusion and frustration. Too many employees said, 'We are constantly pulled in different directions.'"[95]

CSBS is a national organization that was founded in 1902 to advance the professionalism of state banking departments. The organization has evolved to facilitate a nationwide system of coordination among state and federal financial regulators. The growing mortgage-lending crisis led the CSBS in September 2006 to create the Nationwide Multi-State Licensing System and Registry (NMLS), the system of record for nondepository, financial services licensing or registration. In 2008, Congress passed the SAFE Act, requiring that all states license mortgage originators through the NMLS. The system provides a way for the states to manage additional licenses for money transmitters and the debt-collection and consumer-finance industries.

Ten years later, CSBS came to an inflection point. The rapid growth of its NMLS meant that one-third of its employees worked in IT. CSBS's strategy called for implementing Vision 2020, a plan intended to design and execute a high-tech transformation of how states license and supervise nonbanks (a still often paper-based process).

As Jo Ann Barefoot, the CEO of Barefoot Innovation Group and a senior fellow emerita at Harvard University, said in an interview with CSBS president and CEO John Ryan: "I think CSBS is very imaginative, and I think the 2020 effort deserves its 'visionary' labeling. CSBS is a century-old body and it is, after all, a body of regulators. . . . I think other regulators can learn a lot from watching this model, both in how to design new systems and how to build buy-in from a complex set of stakeholders."[96]

To assess CSBS's culture, the organization first asked its senior leaders to describe the culture they wanted to have, then measured the gap against the survey results coming back from employees. Ryan recalls the impact of the results: "This was a wake-up call for me, personally, and for my executive team. To reach our goals, we need to attract and retain talent, and we need to make sure the talented people we have are fully engaged. Clearly, we're just not allowing them to do all that they want to do. Anyone can develop the technology, ultimately it's the people that make the difference."[97]

To strengthen the culture and improve engagement scores, Haire relied explicitly on the Work Systems Model. To pull the Organization Lever, CSBS created a Culture Action Team (CAT) composed of employees from different areas and at various levels across the business, ranging from senior executives to administrative assistants. The CAT created and then implemented a culture action plan. The CAT maintained stakeholder input and involvement in the change effort. The group's plan focused on improving the CSBS experience in four areas: decision making (Decision Allocation), prioritization (Task), organizational values and behavior (People), and staff meeting redesign (Organization).

To pull the Decision Allocation Lever, the CAT brought in Cassie to introduce the RACI[98] tool to the organization. CSBS trained everyone on staff, including the leadership team, and created "super users" in each department (the training also pulled the People Lever). Haire said that "we wanted to approach decision making in two ways, clarifying how and where decisions are made, and next addressing the feedback that decisions are made at too high a level. We needed a common language to have these conversations with one another, and RACI provided that."[99]

The CAT created a subgroup specifically to address the issue of prioritization and competing demands. The issue was exacerbated by the fact that the organization tended to work in silos, with demands coming independently from different parts of the business. To address this, the CAT pulled the Task Lever and recommended that senior leadership identify five organizational priorities. Each priority was then expressed in a strategic framework: Objectives, Goals, Strategies, and Measures.

The CAT also created a subgroup to work on restructuring staff meetings (pulling the Organization Lever). Up until this point, each department reported on its work at a weekly all-staff meeting, reinforcing the identity of the silos. The subgroup redesigned the all-staff meeting with activity reported by organizational priority. Since all of the priorities involve working across departments, the meeting reports modeled cross-functional collaboration, each report involving people from across the organization.

CSBS pulled the Rewards Lever, ensuring that members of the CAT were rewarded for their work on the team. Team participation factored into their performance appraisals and their compensation bonuses, a best practice for cross-functional team work, which often relies on "volunteers" who spend time away from their department commitments with little acknowledgment.

Eighteen months later, CSBS resurveyed and was certified as a "Great Place to Work" by the agency that conducts the largest study of workplace excellence and employee engagement, with a 79% rating.[100] Only about half of GPTW clients achieve the average positivity ratings on their culture surveys that CSBS did.[101]

"We introduced the right tools and the right structure," Ryan said. "Creating a vision of where we wanted to go, aligning the levers and working on multiple things at the same time has been very powerful."[102]

Conclusion

Organizations are huge, complex systems of behaviors. Therefore, leaders who focus on changing behavior markedly increase their odds of successfully changing organizations. The good news for leaders is that behaviors are, in fact, immensely malleable. Human behavior twists and shifts. Immense behavioral variations over millennia bear witness to our marvelous capacity to adapt to the changing world around us. Our ability to adapt to our environment, be it physical or virtual, still impresses. In organizations, the "environment" means the work environment, which is characterized by eight aspects. A change leader who converts those aspects into Change Levers will significantly increase the odds for successful change.

To repeat: We believe that big, radical change can actually prove easier to create and adapt to than incremental change—but only when that big change is *clear* and the work systems *aligned*. Too often we see lots of small or incremental changes, none of them bold enough to be successful, competing against one another for scarce resources and all occurring in a system emitting confusing and contradictory messages. People try to interpret the noise and end up shrugging. Doing things the "old way" ends up being easier than trying to reconcile the competing messages.

How does a change leader clearly align the work systems? It comes back to the two tenets we laid out in chapter 1:

1. Focus on the behaviors you want from people.
2. Design the work environment to foster those behaviors.

The 8 Levers of Change will help a change leader build a work environment that creates the desired behavior. Yet, don't forget to go far enough: You must change enough of the work environment to change how people experience it. Successful change means pulling at least four of the 8 Levers of Change.

Our world—full of uncertainty, innovation, opportunity, and peril—requires much from leaders and followers. Leaders seek to recruit disciples to drive change. Disciples often want the change. They can see the need at ground level. But followers also want and deserve something else: *a fighting chance*, and change leaders should want no less for them. As Napoleon said, "Soldiers generally win battles; generals get credit for them."[103]

Change in a large organization likely means transforming the behavior of thousands, even tens of thousands, of people spread across numerous divisions and multiple continents. With an executive's support, a disciple of change may receive attention in the boardroom; but the deeper within an organization she attempts change, the greater the importance of the local environment. And the farther from Rome that a change agent labors, the less value the emperor's words carry. The new work behaviors need to fit the world faced at work.

The change disciple will have to work within the total work environment of how people are actually organized: the skills, information, and tools at hand; the people with whom she interacts; the protocols and allocation of decision-making authority that guide her actions; and the rewards or punishments that come to her based on measurement. In short, the change disciple will have to deal with the work systems that compose people's work environment, the reality that people see every day at and around their offices or workstations. This local environment shapes local behaviors. A disciple who tries to initiate change at odds with the local reality will almost certainly fail.

Relapsing or recidivism presents a challenge anywhere that advocated behavior does not fit environmental demands. Telling people, for example, to concentrate on cross-unit quality when their environment tells them to concentrate on within-unit volume means promoting a change that doesn't make sense. This then generates a conflict that lessens both people's willingness to alter their behavior and, simultaneously, their tolerance of the change disciple himself. A change disciple who applies increasing amounts of personal pressure in the face of such a disconnect between change message and local reality, especially if he employs punitive actions such as disciplining or firing, will precipitate a choice among employees: Act as the disciple wishes and have the system punish you, or act as the system wishes and have the disciple punish you. Given such a choice, the locals will likely bet on the system and against the change disciple. They will move to marginalize, then neutralize, and, if necessary, eliminate the disciple.

Sending change disciples out to do hard labor without concomitant attention by leaders to work systems strands those disciples and sets them up to fail. That failure costs leaders and disciples alike. Failure to change the work environment therefore amounts to a breach of fiduciary responsibility by the leadership, because it leads predictably to squandered resources. Such failure also qualifies as immoral because of what it does to human beings, especially to the disciples of change.

And failed change saps organizations and their members of time and energy. The emergence of "change fatigue" as a label bespeaks the potential effects of the onslaught of change, especially change inadequately considered and too often failed. Exhausted individuals lack resilience and combined they make for an organization that lacks resilience, even as the world about it demands more. Successful change requires thoughtful consideration of both what change to pursue and how to pursue it. Change leaders need to put in the thought time to make sense of the what and the how of change for themselves and for those they would change. A good conceptual framework can help.

We have offered the Work Systems Model as such a framework. It has helped leaders across industries, organizational levels, and multiple decades to do well by their organizations, by the disciples of change, and, ultimately, by themselves. It has helped them beat the odds against successful change. We hope that you, regardless of your industry or title, find that it helps you at least as much as it helped them.

Acknowledgments

This book sits atop decades of work and the instruction and collaboration of scores of people. Many talented professionals—professors, writers, and consultants—have shaped our respective studies and learning at Harvard College, Yale University, Westinghouse, CFAR, The Coxe Group, and The Wharton School.

Cassie would particularly like to thank her colleagues at CFAR for two decades of their wisdom and partnership, and Mark Schneider, MD, MBA, for his insight and inspiration.

Greg and Cassie offer a special thanks to Janice Rowland for her tireless research, organization, and project management. She invested hundreds of hours in this book and, in nearly countless, very practicable ways, made it possible. We would also like to thank Devin Wachs for her scrupulous work on the text. We most sincerely thank the team at Wharton School Press for their original interest and enduring faith in this project and their valuable contributions to the book. In particular, Steve Kobrin and Shannon Berning helped make this book possible in the first instance and then better and better in scores of subsequent instances. This revised edition benefited notably from the close attention of Shannon Berning and Brett LoGiurato of Wharton School Press.

Cassie would like to thank her daughters, Claire and Katie, for their love, friendship, and faith in her. She would like to thank Bruce for a lifetime of friendship and, of course, for the girls, and her husband, Ben, for his unwavering love and support through thick and thin.

Greg, for his part, turns to his wife and says, "Thank you. Thank you for all of it, including tolerating my distant, lost in thought, 'much less fun' self who wandered through our home during the various bouts of actually writing this book."

Finally, Greg and Cassie each have worked and continue to work with dedicated, talented clients. They have shared struggles, failures, and triumphs of changing their organizations. So many looked at the central component of this book, the Work Systems Model, and said, "That's useful. Say more." That validation, that encouragement as much as anything else, yielded this book. Thank you.

Notes

1 Kurt Wagner, "Twitter Stock Is at a Three-Year High. What Is Going On?" Vox, June 13, 2018, https://www.vox.com/2018/6/13/17455464/twitter-jack-dorsey-stock-growth-explained-profitability (accessed October 4, 2019); Joshua Topolsky, "The End of Twitter," *New Yorker*, January 29, 2016, https://www.newyorker.com/tech/annals-of-technology/the-end-of-twitter (accessed October 4, 2019).

2 Alex Kantrowitz, "How Twitter Made the Tech World's Most Unlikely Comeback," BuzzFeed News, June 21, 2018, https://www.buzzfeednews.com/article/alexkantrowitz/how-twitter-made-the-tech-worlds-most-unlikely-comeback (accessed October 4, 2019).

3 John Rampton, "What Any Company Can Learn from Twitter's Comeback," *Entrepreneur*, June 26, 2018, https://www.entrepreneur.com/article/315605 (accessed October 4, 2019).

4 Wagner, "Twitter Stock."

5 Kantrowitz, "How Twitter."

6 Gregory P. Shea and Robert Gunther, *Your Job Survival Guide: A Manual for Thriving in Change* (Upper Saddle River, NJ: FT Press, 2009).

7 Joseph A. Schumpeter, *Capitalism, Socialism, and Democracy*, 3rd ed. (New York: Harper & Row, 1950).

8 Klaus Schwab, *The Fourth Industrial Revolution* (Geneva, Switzerland: World Economic Forum, 2016).

9 Roger G. Ackerman and Gary L. Neilson, "Partnering for Results: A Case Study of Re-engineering, the Corning Way," *Strategy+Business*, April 1, 1996, https://www.strategy-business.com/article/14910 (accessed October 4, 2019); Carolyn Aiken and Scott Keller, "The Irrational Side of Change Management," *McKinsey Quarterly*, no. 2 (April 2009): 101–109; Ronald N. Ashkenas, "Beyond the Fads: How Leaders Drive Change with Results," *Human Resource Planning* 17, no. 2 (June 1, 1994): 25–44; Philip Atkinson, "Managing Resistance to Change," *Management Services*, April 1, 2005; Hans Henrick Jørgensen, Lawrence Owen, and Andreas Neus, "Making Change Work," IBM Corporation, October 2008, https://www.ibm.com/downloads/cas/ZGOKYPNL (accessed October 5, 2019); Pivotal Resources, "Research Finds Almost Half of Change Initiatives at U.S. Corporations Are Failing to Meet Goals," February 5, 2008, https://www.pivotalresources.com/about/press-releases/failing-to-meet-goals

.html (accessed October 4, 2019); John Darragh and Andrew Campbell, "Why Corporate Initiatives Get Stuck," *Long Range Planning* 34, no. 1 (February 2001): 33–52; Pat Zigarmi and Judd Hoekstra, "Leadership Strategies for Making Change Stick," Ken Blanchard Companies, 2019, https://resources.kenblanchard.com /whitepapers/leadership-strategies-for-making-change-stick (accessed October 5, 2019); and Marcia W. Blenko, Michael C. Mankins, and Paul Rogers, "The Decision-Driven Organization," *Harvard Business Review*, June 2010, http://hbr .org/2010/06/the-decision-driven-organization/ar/1 (accessed October 4, 2019).

10 Simon Blackburn, Sarah Ryerson, Leigh Weiss, Sarah Wilson, and Carter Wood, "How Do I Implement Complex Change at Scale?," McKinsey & Company, May 2011, https://www.mckinsey.com/~/media/mckinsey/dotcom/client_service /public%20sector/pdfs/how_do_i_implement_complex_change_at_scale.ashx (accessed October 4, 2019).

11 Niki Goodridge, "Only 15% of Organizations Succeed in Transforming Their Cultures," Institute for Corporate Productivity (i4cp), March 21, 2019, https:// www.i4cp.com/press-releases/only-15-of-organizations-succeed-in -transforming-their-cultures (accessed October 4, 2019).

12 Gregory P. Shea, "Leading Change," in *Medicine and Business: Bridging the Gap*, ed. Sheldon Rovin (Gaithersburg, MD: Aspen Publishers, 2001), 47. The Work Systems Model is copyrighted by Shea and Associates, Inc.

13 Eric Trist and Ken Bamforth, "Some Social and Psychological Consequences of the Longwall Method of Coal Getting," *Human Relations* 4 (1951): 3–38.

14 Names in the Halloran case study were changed to protect identities. The information comes from interviews with Cassie Solomon and the client in 2008.

15 John Tierney, "Be It Resolved," *New York Times*, January 5, 2012, www.nytimes .com/2012/01/08/sunday-review/new-years-resolutions-stick-when-willpower-is -reinforced.html (accessed October 4, 2019).

16 Interview with Halloran employee, 2008.

17 Correspondence with Göran Carstedt, August 2012.

18 Carmen Nobel, "Are You a Strategist?," Harvard Business School Working Knowledge, July 16, 2012, http://hbswk.hbs.edu/pdf/item7022.pdf (accessed October 4, 2019).

19 Stephen Denning, *The Leader's Guide to Storytelling: Mastering the Art and Discipline of Business Narrative*, 2nd ed. (San Francisco: Jossey-Bass, 2011).

20 Russell Ackoff, Jason Magidson, and Herbert Addison, *Idealized Design: Creating an Organization's Future* (Upper Saddle River, NJ: Wharton School Publishing, 2006).

21 George S. Day and Gregory P. Shea, "Grow Faster by Changing Your Innovation Narrative," *MIT Sloan Management Review* 60, no. 2 (Winter 2019): 26–32.

22 Nick Bunkley, "Joseph Juran, 103, Pioneer in Quality Control, Dies," *New York Times*, March 3, 2008, https://www.nytimes.com/2008/03/03/business/03juran .html (accessed October 4, 2019).

23   James Legge, *The Chinese Classics: Life and Teachings of Confucius* (London: N. Trubner, 1869), 197.

24   Ker Than, "Did Evolution Make Our Eyes Stand Out?," LiveScience, NBCNews .com, November 8, 2006, http://www.nbcnews.com/id/15625720/ns/technology _and_science-science/t/did-evolution-make-our-eyes-stand-out/ (accessed October 5, 2019).

25   Ashton Applewhite, Tripp Evans, and Andrew Frothingham, "And I Quote," in *The Definitive Collection of Quotes, Sayings*, rev. ed. (New York: St. Martin's Press, 2003), 57.

26   Lee Ross, "The Intuitive Psychologist and His Shortcomings: Distortions in the Attribution Process," in *Advances in Experimental Social Psychology*, ed. Leonard Berkowitz (New York: Academic Press, 1977), 184.

27   Dan Lander, "The Creativity Paradox," *UniSA Business*, no. 11 (November 2017), https://unisabusinessschool.edu.au/magazine/11/the-creativity-paradox/ (accessed October 4, 2019).

28   Trevor Hastie, Robert Tibshirani, and Jerome Friedman, *The Elements of Statistical Learning: Data Mining, Inference, and Prediction*, 2nd ed. (New York: Springer, 2009), vii.

29   Kantrowitz, "How Twitter."

30   Interview with Meg Haley, July 8, 2019.

31   Interview with Haley.

32   Interview with Haley.

33   Interview with Haley.

34   Interview with Haley.

35   Interview with Haley.

36   Twitter, "Q2 2019 Letter to Shareholders," July 26, 2019, 2–10, https://s22.q4cdn .com/826641620/files/doc_financials/2019/q2/Q2-2019-Shareholder-Letter.pdf (accessed October 4, 2019).

37   Erik Brynjolfsoon and Lorin M. Hitt, "Beyond Computation: Information Technology, Organizational Transformation and Business Performance," *Journal of Economic Perspectives* 14, no. 4 (Fall 2000): 24.

38   Lauren Joseph, "5 Burning Questions about Using Artificial Intelligence to Prevent Blindness," STAT, July 17, 2019, https://www.statnews.com/2019/07/17 /artificial-intelligence-to-prevent-blindness/ (accessed October 4, 2019).

39   Stephen R. Benoit, Bonnielin Swenor, Linda S. Geiss, Edward W. Gregg, and Jinan B. Saaddine, "Eye Care Utilization among Insured People with Diabetes in the U.S., 2010–2014," *Diabetes Care* 42, no. 3 (March 2019): 427–433, https://doi .org/10.2337/dc18-0828 (accessed October 4, 2019).

40   Joseph, "5 Burning Questions."

41   Interview with Michael Abramoff, July 18, 2019.

42   Interview with Abramoff; Tracy Schaaf, "IDx Technologies: AI Meets Market Access with a Breakthrough Diabetic Retinopathy Detection Device," Medtech Strategist Market Pathways, https://www.mystrategist.com/market-pathways /article/idx_ai_meets_market_access_with_a_breakthrough_diabetic _retinopathy_detection_device_kmb.html (accessed October 4, 2019).

43   Interview with Abramoff.

44   Susan Shepard, "Autonomous AI Device Receives Historic CPT Code," Medical Device and Diagnostic Industry (MD+DI), July 31, 2019, https://www .mddionline.com/autonomous-ai-device-receives-historic-cpt-code (accessed October 4, 2019).

45   Schaaf, "IDx Technologies."

46   Schaaf, "IDx Technologies."

47   Joseph, "5 Burning Questions."

48   American Medical Association, "Policy: Augmented Intelligence in Health Care," 2019, 3, https://www.ama-assn.org/system/files/2019-08/ai-2018-board -policy-summary.pdf (accessed October 4, 2019).

49   Interview with Abramoff.

50   Shepard, "Autonomous AI Device."

51   Jan W. Rivkin, Dorothy Leonard, and Gary Hamel, "Change at Whirlpool Corporation (A)" (Harvard Business School Publishing, 9-705-462, rev. March 6, 2006, 1), www.hbsp.harvard.edu.

52   Rivkin, Leonard, and Hamel, "Change at Whirlpool Corporation (A)," 1.

53   Michael Arndt, "How Whirlpool Defines Innovation," interview with Nancy Snyder by Michael Arndt, *BusinessWeek Online*, March 6, 2006, 14.

54   Arndt, "How Whirlpool Defines Innovation," 14.

55   Arndt, "How Whirlpool Defines Innovation," 14.

56   The Conference Board, "HR's Role in Building a Culture of Innovation," *Executive Action Series*, no. 159, September 2005.

57   Jan W. Rivkin, Dorothy Leonard, and Gary Hamel, "Change at Whirlpool Corporation (B)" (Harvard Business School Publishing, 9-705-463, rev. March 6, 2006, 6), www.hbsp.harvard.edu.

58   Rivkin, Leonard, and Hamel, "Change at Whirlpool Corporation (B)," 6.

59   Arndt, "How Whirlpool Defines Innovation," 1.

60   Whirlpool Corporation, *2018 Annual Report*, 2019, 2, https://s22.q4cdn.com /226840148/files/doc_financials/annual/2018/Whirlpool_2018AR_FINAL.pdf (accessed October 4, 2019).

61   Whirlpool Corporation, *2018 Annual Report*, 9.

62 Disney Institute, *Be Our Guest: Perfecting the Art of Customer Service* (New York: Disney Editions, 2011), 5.

63 Brooks Barnes, "In Customer Service Consulting, Disney's Small World Is Growing," *New York Times*, April 22, 2012, https://www.nytimes.com/2012/04/22/business/media/in-business-consulting-disneys-small-world-is-growing.html (accessed October 4, 2019).

64 Disney Institute, *Be Our Guest*, 183.

65 Disney Institute, *Be Our Guest*, 49.

66 Disney Institute, *Be Our Guest*, 23.

67 Disney Institute, *Be Our Guest*, 23.

68 Jeff Kober, "Disney Service Basics," *Mouse Planet*, November 29, 2007, www.mouseplanet.com/6978/Disney_Service_Basics (accessed October 4, 2019).

69 Barnes, "In Customer Service Consulting."

70 Rebecca A. Clay, "How Portugal Is Solving Its Opioid Problem," *Monitor on Psychology* 49, no. 9 (October 2018), https://www.apa.org/monitor/2018/10/portugal-opioid (accessed October 4, 2019); Nicholas Kristof, "How to Win a War on Drugs," *New York Times*, September 22, 2017, https://www.nytimes.com/2017/09/22/opinion/sunday/portugal-drug-decriminalization.html (accessed October 4, 2019); Johann Hari, "Everything You Think You Know about Addiction Is Wrong," TEDGlobalLondon, June 2015, https://www.ted.com/talks/johann_hari_everything_you_think_you_know_about_addiction_is_wrong (accessed October 4, 2019).

71 Kristof, "How to Win a War on Drugs."

72 Lipi Roy, "'It Starts with Mindset': What Portugal's Drug Policy Experts Taught Me about Addiction Treatment," *Forbes*, August 31, 2018, https://www.forbes.com/sites/lipiroy/2018/08/31/its-starts-with-mindset-what-portugals-drug-policy-experts-taught-me-about-addiction-treatment/ (accessed October 4, 2019).

73 Roy, "'It Starts with Mindset.'"

74 Roy, "'It Starts with Mindset.'"

75 Hari, "Everything You Think."

76 Clay, "How Portugal Is Solving."

77 Kristof, "How to Win."

78 Alan Deutschman, "Change or Die," *Fast Company*, May 1, 2005, www.fastcompany.com/52717/change-or-die (accessed October 4, 2019).

79 Sara R. Govil, Gerdi Weidner, Terri Merritt-Worden, and Dean Ornish, "Socioeconomic Status and Improvements in Lifestyle, Coronary Risk Factors, and Quality of Life: The Multisite Cardiac Lifestyle Intervention Program," *American Journal of Public Health* 99, no. 7 (July 2009), https://ajph.aphapublications.org/doi/full/10.2105/AJPH.2007.132852 (accessed October 4,

2019); Ornish Lifestyle Medicine, "Agents of Change," https://www.ornish.com /site-certification/ (accessed October 4, 2019).

80 Deutschman, "Change or Die."

81 Fred R. Shapiro, *The Yale Book of Quotations* (Hartford, CT: Yale University Press, 2006), 356.

82 Cynthia Montgomery, *The Strategist: Be the Leader Your Business Needs* (New York: HarperBusiness, 2012), 2–3.

83 Peggy Holman, Tom Devane, Steven Cady, and Associates, *The Change Handbook: The Definitive Resource on Today's Best Methods for Engaging Whole Systems*, 2nd ed. (San Francisco: Berrett-Koehler, 2007), xii.

84 Crunchbase, "Viacom: Overview," https://www.crunchbase.com/organization /viacom#section-acquisitions (accessed October 4, 2019).

85 Cynthia Littleton, "Inside Bob Bakish's Aggressive Turnaround Plan for Viacom," *Variety*, December 11, 2018, https://variety.com/2018/biz/features/bob -bakish-viacom-turnaround-1203085842/ (accessed October 4, 2019).

86 Interview with Janice Gatti, June 21, 2019.

87 Interview with Julia Phelps, July 10, 2019.

88 Cynthia Littleton, "Viacom Launches Spark Internal Summit with Eye on Corporate Culture," *Variety*, February 11, 2019, https://variety.com/2019/biz /news/viacom-spark-internal-summit-corporate-culture-1203135296/ (accessed October 4, 2019).

89 Interview with Gatti.

90 Interview with Phelps.

91 Interview with Phelps.

92 Edmund Lee, "CBS and Viacom to Reunite in Victory for Shari Redstone," *New York Times*, August 13, 2019, https://www.nytimes.com/2019/08/13/business/cbs -viacom-merger.html (accessed October 4, 2019).

93 Goodridge, "Only 15% of Organizations."

94 Edgar Schein, *Organizational Culture and Leadership*, 5th ed. (Hoboken, NJ: John Wiley & Sons, 2017), 338.

95 CSBS Culture Assessment Results presentation, 2017; interview with Kelly Haire, August 8, 2019.

96 Jo Ann Barefoot, "Banks and Community: CSBS President John Ryan," Barefoot Innovation Group, August 7, 2017, https://www.jsbarefoot.com/podcasts/2017/8 /7/banks-and-community-csbs-president-john-ryan (accessed October 4, 2019).

97 Interview with John Ryan, January 24, 2019.

98 For more information on RACI, see www.RACISolutions.com.

99 Interview with Haire.

100 John Ryan, email message to Cassie Solomon, September 21, 2019; Great Place to Work, "Conference of State Bank Supervisors," https://www.greatplacetowork.com/certified-company/7011500 (accessed October 4, 2019).

101 Ryan, email message to Solomon.

102 Interview with Ryan.

103 Napoleon Guide, "Napoleon on War," http://www.napoleonguide.com/maxim_war.htm (accessed October 4, 2019).

Index

Page numbers in italics refer to figures.

Endnote references include page number, the letter "n," and note number.

About the Authors

Gregory P. Shea, PhD, consults, researches, writes, and teaches in the areas of organizational and individual change and leadership. He is adjunct professor of management at the Wharton School of the University of Pennsylvania and of its Aresty Institute of Executive Education, senior fellow at Wharton School's Center for Leadership and Change, adjunct senior fellow at the Leonard Davis Institute of Health Economics at Wharton, president of Shea and Associates, Inc., and senior consultant at CFAR. His awards include an Excellence in Teaching Award from Wharton. He is a member of the Academy of Management and the American Psychological Association. He frequently cohosts Wharton Business Radio's *In the Workplace* and has numerous podcasts and articles on Knowledge@ Wharton.

Shea's writing has appeared in such journals as the *Sloan Management Review, Journal of Applied Management, Journal of Applied Behavior Science, Journal of Conflict Resolution, British Journal of Social Psychology, Journal of Management Development*, and *Nursing Administration Quarterly*. He has also served as contributing editor to or reviewer for various professional journals.

Shea coauthored *Your Job Survival Guide: A Manual for Thriving in Change*. He is a magna cum laude, Phi Beta Kappa graduate of Harvard College and holds an MSc in management studies from the London School of Economics and an MA, MPhil, and PhD in administrative science from Yale University.

Cassie A. Solomon teaches leaders and organizations how to design and implement successful change. She is the president and founder of The New Group Consulting, Inc. Before starting her own company, she spent 16 years with CFAR. Cassie is the author of a study of the successful adoption of new technology for the National Academies. She has taught health-care executives at Wharton's Leonard Davis Institute and teaches change management to executives at Wharton's Aresty Institute. She is the creator of RACI Solutions, a method devoted to applying the RACI tool to help leaders strengthen cross-functional teams and horizontal leadership in their organizations and networks. She is a certified futurist and an ardent student of the impact of new technology on the future of work. Cassie is an alumna of Yale University and the Wharton School of Business.

About Wharton School Press

Wharton School Press, the book publishing arm of The Wharton School of the University of Pennsylvania, was established to inspire bold, insightful thinking within the global business community.

Wharton School Press publishes a select list of award-winning, bestselling, and thought-leading books that offer trusted business knowledge to help leaders at all levels meet the challenges of today and the opportunities of tomorrow. Led by a spirit of innovation and experimentation, Wharton School Press leverages groundbreaking digital technologies and has pioneered a fast-reading business book format that fits readers' busy lives, allowing them to swiftly emerge with the tools and information needed to make an impact. Wharton School Press books offer guidance and inspiration on a variety of topics, including leadership, management, strategy, innovation, entrepreneurship, finance, marketing, social impact, public policy, and more.

Wharton School Press also operates an online bookstore featuring a curated selection of influential books by Wharton School faculty and Press authors published by a wide range of leading publishers.

To find books that will inspire and empower you to increase your impact and expand your personal and professional horizons, visit *wsp.wharton.upenn.edu.*

About the Wharton School

Founded in 1881 as the world's first collegiate business school, the Wharton School of the University of Pennsylvania is shaping the future of business by incubating ideas, driving insights, and creating leaders who change the world. With a faculty of more than 235 renowned professors, Wharton has 5,000 undergraduate, MBA, executive MBA, and doctoral students. Each year 18,000 professionals from around the world advance their careers through Wharton Executive Education's individual, company-customized, and online programs. More than 99,000 Wharton alumni form a powerful global network of leaders who transform business every day.

www.wharton.upenn.edu

CPSIA information can be obtained
at www.ICGtesting.com
Printed in the USA
JSHW032259060721
16645JS00004B/154